Bricks and mortals

Sixty years in property

By David Bedford

BRICKS AND MORTALS

ISBN 978-0-9931108-8-7.

Edited by The Writing House Ltd
and printed by Gipping Press Ltd.

To my wife, Sadie

Sadie started painting classes just before I began work on my book, this recent work shows how far she has progressed during her husband's "authors' purdah "

Foreword

In my twenty years with Countrywide, I worked with a great many outstanding estate agents but few, if any, could match the all-round flair and achievement that David Bedford demonstrated over his six decades in the business in East Anglia.

I worked with him for many happy years in the 1970's. Quite remarkably, many of the management information controls he introduced when he had just four or five offices were so forward-thinking that I took them with me to Countrywide, where they were as effective when applied across 1,100 offices nationwide as they had been across the original Bedfords empire in Norfolk.

David taught me much. I have never had the wonderful personal charisma that enables him to mix in any level of society and, even today, many years after "retiring," still attracts wonderful sale instructions to Bedfords, but the skills he shared have been a major help in my own personal career, and I'm proud to have kept both him and his wife Sadie as dear friends.

Writing this book has been a real labour of love for David and I know it will be enjoyed, not just by the hundreds of property professionals who know him well, but by many others who will be touched both by his humility and by his passionate enthusiasm for his business, his family and East Anglia.

I am honoured to have been able to pen this brief introduction.

Harry Hill, Former CEO of
Countrywide, March 2016

Contents

Preface

Looking back, it's clear that I have been a member of a lucky generation. We haven't been forced to go to war. Regardless of our qualifications, we found it easy to get a job. It wasn't too difficult to buy one's first house, and prices have rocketed since. Either directly or indirectly, this has given most of us a good pension to secure our retirement.

It was the long night of Saturday 17th December 2011 that, ultimately, convinced me to set the details of my life down on paper. I was about to set off for what I suspected would be another stressful afternoon at Portman Road watching Ipswich Town lose, so that might have been the final straw but, at lunchtime, I suffered a minor stroke. With tingling all down my left side, I guessed I had a problem. Sadie was out, so I dialled 999. The paramedic was with me in five minutes and, thanks to him and the ambulance crew, I was at West Suffolk Hospital just half an hour after making the call. Thanks to our excellent National Health Service, even at a weekend, I "dodged the bullet" and was released the following Monday afternoon.

It would be another year or two before I started work on what, eventually, would become "Bricks & Mortals." I wrote the book to chart some of the changes I have experienced in my lifetime – not only in the property world (I bought my first property in 1960 for £800 with a 90 percent mortgage!) but also in East Anglia's business and social landscape.

Much of the book is about the business that bears my name – Bedfords. I would like to place on record my thanks to the hundreds of people who have worked with me since I first set up Bedfords 50 years ago, in 1966. Their contributions made the business the success it is today.

I would also like to thank the people who helped me in the production of this book: Diane Plester and Michelle Tyler for deleting all the "umms and ahhs" from the numerous tapes I dictated, Hilary Lynn for proofreading the copy, the team at The Writing House for their help with editing and Bob Cuff of Gipping Press for producing "Bricks & Mortals."

I hope you enjoy my book!

David Bedford, March 2016

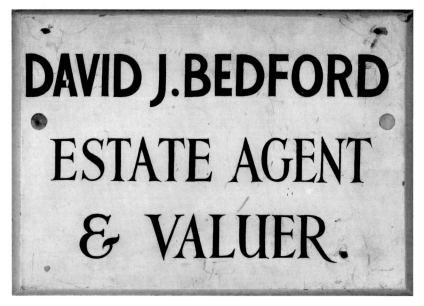

Swaffham, 1966.

BRICKS & MORTALS

Property and People

*Design by Peter Emms who created "The Hollies" sketch
on page 131 over forty years ago.*

DAVID BEDFORD

1955   Start my first job – at Miles Son & Landles in King's Lynn

1957   Move to Arthur Rutter Sons & Company in Bury St Edmunds

1966   Open the first Bedfords office – in Swaffham, Norfolk

1967   Open a branch office in King's Lynn

1968   Open a second branch office in Downham Market

1972   Move to a new headquarters in Swaffham – The Hollies

1972   Open offices in Hunstanton and Fakenham

1974   Acquire the offices of Thetford Property Centre in Watton, Attleborough and Thetford

       Buy the office of a sole practitioner in East Dereham

1976   Take over Noel Abels' offices in Swaffham and Watton

1976   Create a country house department at Bedfords in Swaffham

1977   Publish the first edition of Bedfords' newspaper – *Norfolk Property News*

1978   Acquired Holt office

1979   Dissolve the partnership in Norfolk

       Rebrand the five offices I keep "Bedford – The Estate Agents"

SIXTY YEARS IN PROPERTY

1980   Close the office in Thetford

Sell the offices in Watton and Attleborough

Publish the first edition of Bedfords' full-colour property magazine

1982   Move back to Bury St Edmunds

Acquire the office of E. G. Josling and reopen it as Bedford Country Property Agents

1983   Sell Swaffham and Watton offices to William H. Brown

1984   Go on a fact-finding trip to the United States of America with the National Association of Estate Agents

1987   Sell country property business to Hamptons

Become Hamptons' Regional Managing Director for East Anglia

1990   Leave Hamptons

1991   Re-launch Bedford Country Property Agents in Bury St Edmunds

1995   Open an office in Burnham Market

2003   Open an office in Aldeburgh

2014   Open an office in Woodbridge

2016   Celebrate the 50th anniversary of the launch of my first business

Chapter 1

My Ancestors

Hanging in my office, there's a framed copy of an indenture. Printed on vellum and dated 13 February 1897, it sets out the terms of an agreement between a 15-year-old, John Bedford, and Frank Welham of George Wrycroft & Sons, a firm of builders in St Neots, Huntingdonshire. Over the four years for which the agreement would last, John would be taught the arts of carpentry and joinery. In the first year, he would be paid the princely wage of just 2s 6d (12.5p) a week! He'd earn more later on, of course – 4s 0d (20p) a week in his second year, 5s 6d (27.5p) in his third and 7s 6d (37.5p) in the fourth and final year – but that isn't all that's interesting about the agreement. What we would now call his Contract of Employment included some remarkably interesting conditions:

> *"He should not contract matrimony within the said term, nor play at cards or dice tables, nor haunt taverns or playhouses."*

Employers can't get away with that these days!

As things worked out, John had been free of the indenture just over five years by the time he married Ada, a dressmaker, on 23 March 1906. A report published in the local press on the occasion of their Diamond Wedding celebrations said that it rained, it snowed and the sun shone on their wedding day. Quite a combination!

John – Grandad as I knew him – worked for Wrycroft & Sons for nearly 50 years. When he retired, he turned his favourite hobby of gardening into his main work.

My earliest recollections of him were as a proud exhibitor at the annual St Neots Horticultural Show, where he won numerous prizes for the wonderful well-scrubbed vegetables he grew on his allotment.

Apart from his work with Wrycrofts and the love of his allotment, Grandad Bedford was a founder member of the St Neots Co-operative Society. A letter written at the time of his death in 1972 mentioned the tremendous contribution he made to that organisation over a very long period. Today, the Co-op is virtually owned and controlled by hedge funds, a past chief executive having been arrested on drug charges. Grandad must be turning in his grave!

Elsewhere among his papers, I also found his mortgage repayment book. In July 1949, Grandad took out a loan of £300 against a house in Cambridge Street, St Neots. Generally, he paid off £5 or £6 a month, but in December 1950 he paid off £10. Perhaps he had had a Christmas bonus? The final repayment – £6 9s 11d (about £6.50) – was made in April 1955. I don't think he ever borrowed money again!

--- ooo ---

My father, Frederick John Bedford, was born in 1910.

At 16, he joined his father at George Wrycroft & Sons, where he worked for 18 years before leaving to join the army. That was in May 1943.

Fred married my mother, Clara May Baxter, on 12 August 1933. Both were good tennis players but, rather than play against each other, they often partnered with a local couple, Ellis and Eileen Clark.

By the 1960s, Ellis and Eileen had moved to Thetford. Ellis had become the town clerk and, as "Mr Thetford," became involved in the town's massive expansion as an overspill development for London. As an estate agent working in the area, I came to know him well and spoke to him several times regarding gaps in my understanding of my family's history, the last time just a few weeks before he died in January 2014, aged 97.

My parents' first home was a small bungalow called Hilltop, which they built in the village of Eaton Socon, just across the River Ouse from St Neots. I came along in June 1937, the year after they moved in. This was, of course, just over two years before the commencement of the Second World War.

My sister, Mary, was born a few years later, in April 1943. Staggeringly, just a few weeks after that, Dad went to The Royal Fusiliers' barracks in Bury St Edmunds and joined up. He left George Wrycroft & Sons on 6 May 1943 – just two weeks after my sister Mary was born. Every time I drive past the barracks in Bury, I am reminded of that pivotal event!

Wrycrofts gave Dad a glowing reference, which was nice. I found that among his papers as well.

The last photograph I have of Dad, Mother, Mary and I was, I think, taken in October 1943. Soon afterwards, Dad was sent to Italy and there, on 27 February 1944, he died. I still have the hand-written the Army form that records the event. It reads:

B.104-82, reference CAS/B&H/8501			
NUMBER	14601377	RANK	PRIVATE
NAME	BEDFORD,	REGIMENT	BEDS &
	FREDERICK JOHN		HERTS

Dad was killed in what was known as the Central Mediterranean Theatre of War. Reference CAS on the form, which refers to Cassino, suggests he died there. The battle for Monte Cassino was Britain's bitterest and bloodiest encounter with the German army on any front in World War II, with over a quarter of a million men killed or wounded in the six-month struggle. A letter from a colleague-in-arms called Les to Dad's sister, my Auntie Gladys, says "Fred was killed instantaneously by a mortar bomb and he is buried on the side of a hill with six of his mates."

I was only six-and-a-half years old when Dad died, but I have vague recollections of embarrassing silences and closed doors around the house. While I am sure Dad joined up voluntarily for the best of motives – to serve King and Country – Mother was understandably very bitter, especially as he had left her in charge not just of me, coming up to age six, but of my sister, Mary, who was just a few weeks old.

Over the years, I offered on several occasions to take Mother to Rome to see where Dad died, but she never wanted to go.

Then, in 1994, on the anniversary of the invasion, the television news covered President Clinton's visit to the war graves at Anzio and I decided I really needed to go. My wife, Sadie, and my sister wanted to come, but we decided not to tell Mother, who by this time was suffering from Alzheimer's disease. Instead, we planned to tell her about the trip when we got home.

We had a very emotional weekend in Italy. Sensibly, we got a driver to take us the 100 miles or so to Anzio and on to the cemetery at Casino, where we found Dad's name quite high up on one of the large tombstones. I stretched up with my camera and took a few photographs.

Returning home on the Sunday evening, we had not been in the house ten minutes when James, my middle son, telephoned to say that Granny had had a stroke and was in King's Lynn Hospital. Sadly, she never regained consciousness, so we never got to tell her about our trip.

The final twist of the story was when I had the film from my camera developed. It was then that I spotted that the typeface used on the memorial in Italy was exactly the same as was used in my firm's logo.

All quite eerie really!

Chapter 2

School Days

I started my schooling in St Neots when I was about five years old. I can picture the day in my mind but, to get the details straight, I have had to seek some help from mates who were pupils at about the same time. They include David and Tony Craig, two of my closest friends back then. They lived in Wrycroft Avenue in a house that, given its age, could well have been one my Grandad worked on when he was with Wrycrofts.

The school we went to was in a semi-detached house directly opposite where the Craigs lived. David confirms it was called Hartsbury and was run under the strict control of a Miss Endesbury. Thinking back, I think only two or three rooms in the house were used for schooling, which suggests there couldn't have been many more than 15 pupils. Despite this, we must have received a good basic education: the three of us and David Flint, another great friend, did well enough to gain entrance to a public school – Bedford Modern.

--- ooo ---

We started at Bedford Modern in September 1946. Every day, we would have to catch the bus to travel the 12 miles there to Bedford and the 12 miles back home.

I certainly hadn't won a scholarship, so I am not quite sure how Mother managed to afford to send me to what was a fee-paying school. Times must have been hard but, in 1948, she remarried. My stepfather had a pension from the navy and a reasonable job with the oil company, Shell. They were far from wealthy, but the financial situation must have improved, because I became a boarder at Bedford Modern in 1949. For understandable reasons, I had been somewhat spoilt up to then, so going to a boarding school at the age of 12 was a bit of a shock!

Overall, I have very happy memories of my school days. The discipline was very strict and the conditions were quite spartan, but neither really did us any harm.

When I became a boarder, I shared a dormitory on the top floor with about a dozen other boys. There, each of us had a simple iron bed and a small bedside cupboard. There was a row of washstands down the middle of the room, which we shared, and each of them had a bowl and a large jug of cold water. I remember them particularly well! In the winter, we often had to break the ice off the water before we washed.

There was, however, one big advantage to being on the top floor. On the opposite side of the road, beyond the tennis court, there was a ladies' physical education college. Our building probably looked to be some distance away, so the young ladies there were fairly relaxed when it came to drawing their curtains. After the first exeat, two or three of my pals returned with powerful binoculars that they had borrowed from their parents to pursue their new interest in "bird" watching. As young pubescent boys, it was a hobby we embraced with some considerable enthusiasm!

While most of the boys in each dormitory were about the same age, each had a senior dormitory prefect. Ours was Dicky Jeeps, an exceptional rugby player who went on to play for and captain not just England but, I think, for the Lions. In the event of a misdemeanour, he, like the other dormitory prefects, had considerable authority. He could report you to the house master, or thrash you with three or four strokes of his slipper. If it was a relatively serious offence, boys would usually opt for the slipper as the house master would always administer six strokes of the cane.

--- ooo ---

Academically, I jogged along, but finally I obtained three O Levels, or GCSEs as they would be called these days. Despite coming from three generations of carpenters, my wife can confirm that I am far from skilled when it comes to jobs around the house. But I can't have been completely at a loss with my hands: one of those O Levels was in metalwork!

The school house we lived in was about a mile from the main school. On the way there each morning, we would encounter many blossoming young schoolgirls walking in the opposite direction. The combination of this with the grandstand view my mates and I were enjoying of the physical training college proved quite distracting. Thanks to our "bird" watching, we knew just what was under the tight sweaters we saw each morning!

This brings me to one of the loves of my life: sport.

Like all public schools, Bedford Modern had excellent sporting facilities. In the main, it focused on rugby, cricket and rowing. In the winter term, we all played rugby. I never excelled at the game, but it was quite good fun, especially when there was a match and we had a good tea afterwards. In the summer, there was a choice of cricket or rowing. I opted for rowing, which I enjoyed very much. I was a stroke in the third eight and sometimes promoted to the second eight. In classic style, the rowing coach would be furiously peddling down the river bank of the Ouse shouting "in" and "out," which created quite a lot of giggling among the female admirers who turned out regularly to see us.

The other thing I enjoyed at school was being a member of the Army Corps. Fearing this it might lead me into the army, Mother was never keen.

In the last summer before we left school, Richard Webb, who had become my best mate, Ron Jell and I all went off to army camp in Otterburn, on the Scottish borders. As you might imagine, the regulars in charge gave us a pretty hard time but, in the evenings, we enjoyed a crash course in consuming huge amounts of beer.

A less fond memory of the school was of the food. I'm afraid it was pretty awful. From the day I left, I have never ever eaten swede again! Fortunately, we were allowed to keep a personal jar of jam, or similar, in a cupboard in the hall. That was nice, but some would get forgotten or mislaid and, when rediscovered, would have a fairly active crust on the top!

We were only allowed to go home overnight for the holidays, but we had free time every Sunday. To keep ourselves nourished, Richard or another pal and I would cycle home to St Neots for lunch.

--- ooo ---

When I left school in the summer of 1954, I almost immediately learnt that Chris, my stepfather, had been moved by Shell to King's Lynn. The family would soon be moving to Norfolk.

That summer, I spent a lot of time rowing for St Neots' Rowing Club at various regattas in the region. This made up for the disappointment of leaving school. If I had stayed on, the coach had suggested I might well have gone on to row in the first eight in the Henley Royal Regatta. I had dreamt of doing this for years but, given my unspectacular exam results, I didn't feel I could persuade my parents to pay for another year's school fees just so that I could enjoy the glory of rowing at Henley.

A farmer who lived next door offered me a job helping out with the harvest. This produced a useful income, but I wasn't used to manual work. On the positive side, it did leave me with some stories to tell. When an old threshing machine or tractor-drawn harvester appears in some black-and-white documentary on TV, my grandchildren can't believe it when I tell them "I used to work on one of those."

Mother thought it would be a good idea if I became a policeman. A family friend had a contact with an inspector at Peterborough and I was driven over there for an interview. It took place in the starkest room I had ever seen. The inspector and I sat either side of a very plain desk. For a while, I thought it and the chairs were the only things in the room but, after a while, I noticed a length of wood propped in the corner behind the inspector's chair. It appeared to have dark blotches on it. At the end of the meeting, the inspector asked if I had any questions, so I asked what was propped up against the wall behind him. With a smile on his face, he told me it was evidence – a weapon a worker at the local brick works had used to kill his neighbour the night before.

After that, I returned to the car. On the way home, Mother asked how I got on. Fine, I said, but I didn't think I really wanted to be a policeman.

--- ooo ---

I continued work for the farmer into October. Then on one frosty morning, he sent some fellow workers and myself out to a field to gather Brussels sprouts by hand. That made up my mind: farming was not for me!

Despite Mother expressing her concern that I neither had a job nor any idea what I wanted to do, I really enjoyed that summer and autumn. I was free of the restrictions imposed by school, I was earning money and I was enjoying spending it with pals, going to parties and enjoying female company.

My grandmother lived about a mile from our home, opposite St Neots Golf Club. The club's grounds ran down to the River Ouse where, by the bank, a local doctor and his wife lived with their family in a very pleasant house. The doctor's daughter was five years older than me and very attractive. I enjoyed her company a great deal and spent an increasing number of nights at my grandmother's house so I could take full advantage of it. Grandmother was quite hard of hearing so, unlike Mother, had no idea when I came in. It meant I could enjoy the daughter's company well into the evening without fear of being questioned. I remember her name, but won't mention it here. Suffice to say that, on one of those evenings, she helped me add O-level biology to my list of qualifications. The exam took place in a bunker nearby – a grass one, I think!

---- ooo ---

While a new home was being built for our family, my stepfather was in digs in King's Lynn.

Early that November, Mother insisted that I went there for a week to find myself a job. The ride through The Fens to King's Lynn was quite depressing but, when I got there, I found it to be very pleasant, with a market square and some fine buildings. Back then, there was no sign of the storm clouds that led to the redevelopment of the town in the 1960s.

I strolled down the high street, as I had been told that the Youth Employment Office was on the second floor on the corner of Norfolk Street above Allen & Neale, the local chemist. There, I was greeted with a friendly smile by a lady who I later discovered was called Betty Tompsett.

"What can I do for you, young man?" she said.

Stating the obvious, I said I was looking for a job.

"What sort of job do you want? Do you want to work in an office, or outside?"

I said I didn't really know or care. Armed with this insight, Mrs Tompsett thumbed through her box file of cards – no computers in those days! The first one she plucked out was for a local firm of auctioneers and estate agents – Miles Son & Landles – who were looking for a "junior." An appointment was arranged and I duly went to their office – Blackfriars Chambers in Blackfriars Street – for an interview. I can't remember the meeting itself, but it must have gone well, as I was offered the job at a salary of £4 a week. The rest, as they say, is history!

Chapter 3

Off to Work

I started at Miles Son & Landles on 1 January 1955. New Year's Day wasn't a bank holiday at that time.

I worked in Blackfriars Chambers, the top floor of a substantial Victorian building in the heart of King's Lynn called Blackfriars Hall. The extensive ground floor of the building operated as a furniture sale room. The offices of Miles Son & Landles, the firm I worked for, were on the first floor. I remember them as gloomy – almost Dickensian. Geoffrey Collings, the principal of the firm, was a bit of a Scrooge. The place was lit with dim 40 or 60 watt bulbs and the heating was non-existent! The reason for this was simple. Collings' tenure was, I believe, to be a limited one. After the previous principal, Mr Landles, had died of a heart attack in his late forties, his widow had employed Collings to run the business until such time as her son, William, had left school and could run the business himself. Collings needed to make profits while he could!

The main activities of the firm centred on the sale room, where a sale was held every three weeks or so. The firm also managed properties for clients, some of whom owned whole streets of modest terraced houses in the centre of King's Lynn, many of which have since been demolished. I recall in particular Windsor Road, just off London Road, and South Clough Lane, on the other side of Blackfriars Street from the office. They've been replaced by a swimming pool and a car park.

One of my duties was to collect rents. Averaging between three and four shillings (15p and 20p) a week, they were collected monthly or, in the case of slow payers, sometimes weekly. As I went from door to door, I got used to hearing all manner of excuses from those in arrears, but I was expected to collect at least something from everyone on account. I remember one occasion when I nearly came unstuck. The tenant – a widow – rented a cottage in South Clough Lane. Every time I called, she reminded me that her son was a boxer, pointing to a sideboard full of trophies to prove it. When I pressed her for the rent, her response was usually "my son is upstairs and I'll call him to deal with you." Following a call up the stairs, she usually relented, muttering something along the lines of "he must be asleep" but, on this particular day, what had previously been a charade turned ugly. The son came pounding down the stairs. When his formidable frame filled the doorway, I decided to throw in the towel and beat a hasty retreat! I seem to recall that, not long afterwards, the council started buying up properties in the area. Thank goodness I didn't have to do what they must have done – to evict the tenant and her aggressive son!

Established in 1856 – a fact built into the company's current name, Landles Auctioneers 1856 Ltd – the firm's office also accommodated the King's Lynn Building Society. As was usual among small building societies back then, the members of the board of directors were all partners of local professional firms – solicitors, accountants, local corn merchants, builders and the like. Collings was the secretary, which explained the society's presence in Blackfriars Chambers. But renting out the space wasn't just an act of kindness. Those who held mortgages with the society had to visit the office every month to pay their dues, which gave the firm an advantage when families decided to sell up or move to larger properties. Thirty years later, the banks and building societies decided to exploit similar "synergies" when they went on a spree of buying up estate agents. This had disastrous results for both parties, but more of this later.

The King's Lynn Building Society's method of business could really only be described as feudal. The day after a monthly board meeting, Collings would type up the minutes on an ancient typewriter that lived on top of a safe in his office. In winter months, he did this wearing mittens!

Another of my jobs was to do the filing. Being of a curious nature, I read sections of the minutes. The following gives a flavour of how the Society seemed to conduct its business:

"We have an application from Mr Smith and Miss Jones for a loan of £1,000," announced the secretary.

"Is that the daughter of Fred Jones, the tailor?" asked the local accountant.

"Yes," came the reply followed, I imagine, by a general murmur of approval from those present.

"Well that's alright, then. Approved!"

The board would then move on to an application from another couple – let's call them Mr Robinson and Miss Carter – for a loan of £800. A similar discussion would take place, but it would emerge that they both lived in Loke Road, on the wrong side of the tracks in King's Lynn. That would settle it. "No, I don't think we can help!"

When it came to the item on the agenda regarding arrears, there would typically only be one or two owing a month's back payment. A board member would be delegated to have a quiet word with the offending party's father at the next meeting of the Rotary Club.

Yes, it was feudal, but it worked. The King's Lynn Building Society eventually got taken over by the Peterborough Building Society, which then merged with the Norwich Building Society. In turn, it merged with the Yorkshire Building Society, becoming the second-largest mutual in Britain after the Nationwide. Not bad for an organisation that was once so feudal!

--- 000 ---

Returning to my career, it was explained to me that, if I was to have any future in the business, I would have to be elected to the Chartered Auctioneers and Estate Agents Institute[1]. To achieve this, I would either have to go to university or complete a correspondence course. I discovered that, providing I obtained an O Level in English Language, I could enrol for the correspondence course, so that's what I decided to do.

After studying at the technical college in King's Lynn, I added two further O Levels to my CV in 1956, one of which was in English Language. I signed up as a student member of the

---

[1] The organisation later became part of the Royal Institution of Chartered Surveyors, RICS.

Chartered Auctioneers and Estate Agents Institute straight away, and then for the correspondence course at the College of Estate Management that I needed to get full membership. My enthusiasm wasn't just because I was keen to get on, although I was. At the time, I was of an age at which I could be called up for National Service. By starting on the course, I kicked that into the long grass, much to the relief of my mother!

In parallel with my studies, I renewed my interest in sport.

Collings was a vice president of the West Norfolk Rugby Club, which at that time had just one team, based at The Red Cat – a pub in North Wootton. It played at a pitch nearby.

One day, Collings said he thought it would be a good idea if I became a member. Before I could give an answer, I received a telephone call from the captain asking if I was available to play at home on the coming Saturday. Thinking it would be rude to decline, I agreed.

At the time, the team was mostly made up of farmers who weren't just physically and financially much stronger than me, they were much better rugby players as well. Although I played rugby at school, it wasn't to a high standard. How things have changed! Back in 1955, the club had only one team and the captain had to call me – a relatively poor player – in on a Thursday or Friday to play on the wing and make up the numbers. According its website, the club now runs something like a dozen teams. It clearly has no problem in fielding either regular sides or senior, veteran and youth teams.

Despite feeling outclassed, I enjoyed the sport. The trouble was that a large part of my £4-a-week salary would disappear on a Saturday night in the bar of The Red Cat.

At about this time, I also joined the local Young Conservatives Club, where I met Neville Carter who, as we'll discover later, soon became a life-long friend. A keen hockey player, Neville turned out for the local club, Pelicans, which played at North Runcton near King's Lynn. One weekend when I wasn't playing rugby – quite possibly because West Norfolk Rugby Club had found someone better! – Neville invited me to go to North Runcton to watch a game and have a beer afterwards. Pelicans also only had one team at the time and, as I soon discovered, similar difficulty in fielding a side. When we got to the ground, it soon became clear that someone hadn't turned up. I had never held a hockey stick in my hand before, but I was persuaded to put on some borrowed kit and have a go. I didn't do too badly and enjoyed the game and company afterwards.

Compared with the relatively cosy bar at The Red Cat, Pelicans' club house was an ex-army timber-built building. There weren't any showers – just two tin baths fed by a freestanding water heater. If you were anything other than the first or second person to use a bath, you'd find it full of liquid mud!

The bar was run by a wonderful lady from the village, called Mabel, who also provided the food. Her "signature" dish was a beetroot sandwich – a delicacy that was a source of great amusement. After a snooty Norwich club came to play in "deepest" West Norfolk, it even got a mention in the local paper, The Eastern Daily Press!

Although Collings had offered me my first job, I was never very fond of him, so it was with some trepidation when I informed him that I had decided to play hockey instead of rugby. He didn't seem to mind – probably because he'd had reports of my skill (or lack of it!) on the rugby field.

--- ooo ---

Collings' other great love was The King's Lynn Operatic & Dramatic Society, for which he was a musical director. I can't imagine how he thought it would advance my career, but soon he was urging me to attend rehearsals for its autumn production. As it happened, this was very welcome. I had recently met a young lady who was a member!

Back at work, the regular furniture sales were the highlight of the business as far as I was concerned. On viewing and sale days, a fascinating collection of characters would make their way to Blackfriars Hall, ranging from small-time dealers to aristocracy who had fallen on difficult times.

On the whole, the contents of the sale were pretty average, but, alongside an awful lot of household furniture and worse, they included some decent antiques. A week or two after each sale took place, consignments for the following one would arrive and be placed haphazardly around the main hall. A week before the sale, we would start to sort everything out. The "we" included two other youngsters who worked full-time for the firm, Richard and Archie, and a couple of older part-time employees, one of whom ran a small second-hand shop in North Everard Street. Due to his knowledge, the latter acted as head porter.

There were three distinct areas to each sale: decent furniture and pictures were displayed in the main hall, everything else apart from carpets in the back hall, and carpets on the floor above.

After each sale, there would be lots that remained unsold. Sellers rarely wanted them back, so Richard, Archie and I were paid an extra – I think it was ten shillings (50p) – to work in our lunch hours for a week to chop unsold furniture up with an axe into pieces that were small enough for the dust cart to take away. Recycling only went so far at the time!

Many years later, my wife decided to attend upholstery classes and wanted a Victorian chaise-longue. We attended one of Noel Abel's sales, where I acquired one for about £200 which she quickly reduced to a pile of bits of wood and springs. To be fair, she made a good job of it. It still sits on the landing in our house. Every time I walk past it, I think of the chaise-longue I helped chop up at Blackfriars Hall. There must have been more than a hundred of them!

Bearing in mind the starvation wages we were on, Richard, Archie and I decided to become small-time furniture dealers. One sale day, we purchased several back-room lots under the pseudonym "Carruthers." Over the next week or two, we spent our lunch hours polishing our purchases up before placing them in the prime spot in the front hall, which was just inside the door on the right. For a while, this generated a spectacular increase in our income, but then I fell ill. By then, I had become very frustrated with how the business was run and with its lack of interest in selling, rather than renting, either houses or commercial properties. Collings wouldn't hear anything – and why should he? – but I finished up with an ulcer at the age of 18!

Normally, Archie and I would do the accounts for each furniture sale, producing detailed statements for each client. Most would be paid by cheque, but quite a few expected to be paid in cash including, as it happens, "Mr Carruthers."

While I was away from the office, Mrs Collings came in to help with the accounts. The fear of discovery did little to help my ulcer!

A couple of weeks after one sale, I received a curt letter from Collings saying he would like to see me upon my return to the office to talk about Mr Carruthers' account which, by then, was in credit to the tune of £52. Richard and Archie had received similar invitations and had confessed to our sinful trading so, on my return, we all received a severe reprimand. We all kept our jobs but, as the ringleader, my salary was reduced from £4 to just £3 a week. It was a blow, but one that didn't last for long. Because of his other business, the head porter was allowed to buy and sell, so we immediately made him a partner in our business and carried on as usual!

Chapter 4

Progressive Barn Dance

We lived in an area called Gaywood, which was some distance from the centre of King's Lynn. Having no alternative at the time, I would travel to work by bus, catching it in Queensway at the end of Baldwin Road. The bus continued into Kent Road and Gayton Road before heading into King's Lynn. The passengers were the usual mixture for the time of day – office workers and girls working in various shops.

Every morning, an attractive young girl would board the bus at the Kent Road stop. After getting off at the same stop in King's Lynn as me, she would stride purposefully past Blackfriars Hall to somewhere further into the town.

Unbeknown to me, a bit of matchmaking had been going on back home in Baldwin Road. Eventually, my mother informed me that a near neighbour, Mrs Bream, had told her that her daughter, Jill, would be attending a dance in Gaywood Village Hall the coming Friday evening. I'd been in King's Lynn quite a while by then, but had not met any female company, either in the office or elsewhere, so I thought, "why not?" On the Friday evening, I duly knocked on the neighbour's door. It was opened by Jill, who seemed quite a pleasant girl – big in the right places – and off we went.

Gaywood Village Hall was clearly the place to be on a Friday night. There were lots of people there – among them, the Kent

Road girl. As the evening progressed, there were various dances, including different permutations and groups, so it wasn't until towards the end of the evening that an opportunity to meet her arose. It was announced that the last dance wouldn't just be a barn dance, but a progressive barn dance – one in which participants move forward to take a new partner after a certain number of steps and movements. I invited Jill onto the floor, making sure we were only a few couples away from my target. The dance started and, after a few minutes, I found myself partnering "Miss Kent Road." I quickly introduced myself and discovered that her name was Sadie. The dance duly progressed but, just before the end, I found myself partnering her again. That time, I discovered she was a hairdresser and worked opposite the Post Office.

The dance ended, leaving me wondering how I was going to be able to move things forward. To my surprise, Sadie got on the bus the following morning and sat next to me. But the good news didn't last long. I tried turning on the charm, but she obviously thought that Jill and I were an item. I did get somewhere, though. By the time we got into King's Lynn, I had found out her surname!

--- oOo ---

During 1956, there was a new arrival at Blackfriars Hall. Peter Hart, who was about ten years older than me and qualified as a chartered auctioneer and estate agent, re-joined the firm. He had worked with Collings for a year or two before but, after a broken engagement with a girl in Hunstanton, had left and joined a firm in Essex. This new job didn't work out as Peter hoped and Collings had persuaded him to return.

Peter and I immediately hit it off and became friends. They say that you should never go back and, in Peter's case, it proved true. I am not sure how it came about, but he was soon offered a job by Freddie Laws, the sole principal of a long-established firm in Bury St Edmunds called Arthur Rutter, Sons & Company. Peter decided to accept.

Not long after my salary had been cut following the sale room "scandal," I had several long conversations with Peter which left him in no doubt how disappointed I was about Landles' lack of interest in selling property – something I'd become interested in.

Peter and I kept in touch following his move to Bury and I still have a letter he wrote to me following a trip he made back to King's Lynn. In the letter – it was dated Tuesday 30 October 1956 – he thanked Mother for Sunday lunch and said he'd had a word with Freddie, who had said he'd keep his eyes open for a position for me. He went on to say that there was a slight chance Rutters would be able to offer me something at the end of the year.

It must have been shortly after that when Peter told me that an opening had come up. I asked Mother to drive me to Bury St Edmunds on a Saturday afternoon so I could meet with Freddie Laws at Rutters' office at 86 Guildhall Street. The firm's receptionist had left and Peter had persuaded Freddie that I should replace her in the front office starting on 1 January 1957, doubling up as a sales negotiator.

My relationship with Collings was at a fairly low ebb, so I didn't care what he thought by then. I simply told him I was leaving. He turned quite nasty, telling me that if I left a firm like his – remember, it wasn't actually his – I would finish up sweeping the streets.

So it was that I found myself out of work – and without an income – several weeks before Christmas 1956. Fortunately, my parents still had a few jobs to do to finish off their house, so I built a wall for them in lieu of a present. The bricks were "borrowed" from a building site nearby. I hadn't built a wall before, but I must have been good at it. When I drove past the property recently, it was still standing!

Collings must have continued to fume after I left. I mentioned earlier that, because I was taking a correspondence course, I was excused National Service. When Collings found out I was joining Peter in Bury St Edmunds, this gave him an opportunity to make mischief. On 19 December 1956, I received a letter from someone at the Ministry of Labour and National Service that started "I have been informed by Messrs Miles Sons & Landles of King's Lynn that you left their employment in November 1956." It went on to ask why I had terminated my employment and say that, unless they received a satisfactory reply, I would be called up for National Service within 14 days.

Chapter 5

Off to Bury

I have many good memories of my two years in King's Lynn.

After that first bus ride together, Sadie made a point of not sitting next to me despite my always ensuring the adjoining seat was available. Just before Christmas 1955, I plucked up courage to telephone her. Introducing myself as "the bloke in the duffel coat on the bus," I invited her to the cinema, only to be told that she couldn't make it because she was having her hair done. As she was a hairdresser, this came as a surprise, but Sadie quickly explained that, in the run-up to the holiday, the salon where she worked was completely booked up. A friend was coming round to do her hair at home.

After Christmas, I thought I would give it another try. That time, Sadie accepted my invitation. So it was that, on a freezing January evening, we set off for the Pilot Cinema in King's Lynn to see Gregory Peck in *The Purple Plain*.

The evening went well, but I didn't get a lot of encouragement over the following weeks. Some evenings, I would hover outside the Post Office opposite the salon where she worked, hoping to bump into her after work. Sometimes, this worked but, more often than not, her friends were sent to check if I was there at closing time and she would disappear out of the back door if I was. We did, however, meet at a number of social occasions – in particular, at the Young Conservatives – and over time, our friendship blossomed. By the time I left Miles Son & Landles and was arranging my move to Bury St Edmunds, we had very much become an item. We were both very young and Sadie was desperately upset that this might mean the end of our relationship.

--- ooo ---

You will have noted that I have referred to Collings only by his surname, which reflected my opinion of him.

Collings was obviously sore that Peter Hart had left him for a second time, and my decision to join him just made matters worse. His attempt to torpedo the deferment of my National Service made me very angry, but it was just an irritation. I hadn't given up on the correspondence course, so there was no chance I would be called up. It was Collings' suggestion that I might end up sweeping streets that had a lasting effect. When I arrived in Bury St Edmunds on New Year's Eve 1956, I was determined to succeed in business!

Peter had digs in York Road and had secured me a room with a neighbouring landlady at number 46. It cost £1 17s 6d (about £1.78) a week for bed and breakfast and evening meal.

In anticipation of my new income, I had purchased a motorbike, but when I moved to Bury, Mother drove me there with all my belongings. She was quite emotional about my leaving home – as I suppose all mothers are when their offspring "fly the nest" – and had bought me a stout new pair of shoes and a very smart raincoat to get me started. I don't know what the proper name for the type of coat is, but it was the type worn by army officers in war films.

Mother also bought me a £50 Premium Bond, which she insisted on looking after. Over the next few years, I used the bond as security whenever I was caught short. Mother would lend me what I needed, secure in the knowledge that, if I didn't give the money back, she would cash in the bond.

Having unpacked the car, inspected my room and met my landlady – a very pleasant, homely person who turned out to be a very good cook – Mother left to return to Norfolk. That evening, Peter came round, knocked on the door and informed my landlady that I would need a key as we were going into town!

The Angel Hotel on Angel Hill in Bury St Edmunds is a landmark building and it was there that I spent my first evening in Bury St Edmunds. I remember to this day looking out of the window at the illuminated Abbey Gate. As I have told many people over the years, it was "love at first sight."

I cannot pretend to remember my first day in Guildhall Street, but the first few weeks were a revelation compared with my experience in Norfolk. The atmosphere in the office was wonderful, everybody worked hard (and appeared to enjoy it!) and the clients were in a different league. We were managing farms and country estates rather than the terraced houses on the books in King's Lynn.

For the amount of business, there were relatively few staff. Freddie Laws dealt with all the agricultural matters, helped by his formidable secretary, Miss Brown, who Peter had warned me not to upset. There was a bookkeeper, a couple of secretaries and another assistant. Peter's main duties revolved around sales and valuations.

These days, banks and building societies rely on in-house valuers to decide whether loans should be made. To put it politely, they are "guided" as to the number of mortgages their employers wish to hand out in a given period. Back then, the work was done by local surveyors, who took a more independent view. Peter was one such surveyor, but his main responsibility was to develop and expand the sale of houses. I helped him with this work.

It is hard to believe but, back in those days, the particulars of houses on sale were reproduced using Gestetner copiers – devices that made copies using stencils wrapped around drums. Everything was in black and white, and there wasn't a picture in sight – not even in agents' windows.

"For Sale" boards were equally primitive. On them, you'd find the history of the relevant firm, complete with the date they were established, the fact that they were chartered auctioneers and estate agents, and their full address. The words "For Sale" appeared almost as an afterthought and, in oddly small type, there would be a telephone number that even pedestrians would find hard to read.

At the time, it was only a fortunate few who could buy a car, but the numbers on the roads were increasing pretty fast. Recognising that drivers were more likely to have money to buy houses than people on foot, one of the first things Peter and I did was to design boards that could easily be read from passing cars.

We also changed the size of the boards we used. Traditionally, boards were approximately 15 or 16 inches (about 40cm) square. Made of enamelled steel, they were mounted on wooden posts. If one had blown over, it could easily have decapitated a passerby!

We decided to use rectangular hardboard signs measuring 3ft by 2ft (90cm by 60cm). Each had a timber border and was secured to a post. Printed on paper that we pasted onto the boards, the text was brief and clear:

> **For Sale**
> # RUTTERS
> **Bury St Edmunds 83**

The name of the firm was actually Arthur Rutter, Son & Company. On notepaper and everything else, it continued to appear in full, but Freddie admitted that he knew nothing about selling houses and was happy to leave the design of the signs to us.

We stuck the paper notices onto the boards using what, at the time, was a revolutionary new product – Polycell Paste. And so it was that, from time to time, I had to walk a few yards up the street to the old established ironmongers and general store, Andrews & Plumpton, to buy a packet of Polycell. It was one of those shops that always had more staff than customers, but you could still never get served! They had tills of the kind you only see these days in repeats of *Are You Being Served* – the comedy by David Croft that's set in an old fashioned departmental store called Grace Brothers. One day, as I stood in front of one of these marvellous tills waiting to be served, I suddenly had an urge to use it. With no help in sight, I went behind the counter and helped myself to a packet of paste, turned round and with a flourish pressed the button for two shillings (10p). The tab displaying the amount shot up and the till opened. I dropped a two shilling piece in the till, closed it and left. Glancing halfway up the shop to where Mr Plumpton always stood wearing his wing collar shirt, I saw him pointing at me, asking one of his colleagues if I was a member of staff.

Together with some slightly more imaginative advertising in the Bury Free Press, the boards had a dramatic impact on business. Surprisingly, few of the other well-established firms in the town took much notice. They probably saw us as brash young upstarts.

Quite a number of both Peter's and my friends were young local solicitors working for well-established firms around the town, so our social connections brought in business as well. On Wednesday evenings, we'd go to Young Conservatives; on Thursdays, to Young Farmers. Both met in the Conservative Club – known locally as the Con Club – where the beer was about 7d (about 3p) a pint. It was about 9d (about 5p) a pint in The Angel, so we only went there when we really wanted to impress a young lady.

--- ooo ---

Although my main job was to assist Peter, I quite frequently went out with Freddie Laws. He was the agent for parts of the then Marquis of Bristol's estates in Suffolk and for several other substantial landowners.

Freddie went shooting most weeks in the winter. His diary would typically show at least one day of such "appointments" with people such as Charles Forte, the hotelier, and Peter Hill-Wood, whose family owned Arsenal Football Club. Some of these clients had rather plummy voices. On one occasion, I remember taking a call from one such gentleman who asked to speak to Mr Laws. When I put him through, I told Freddie that "Claude" Fisher was on the line. A few moments later, an apoplectic Miss Brown came through to inform me that it was actually Lord Fisher – one of Freddie's regular shooting partners!

It intrigued me that Freddie could spend so much time away from the office yet do so well in business. I had no interest in shooting at the time but, once I had established my own business, Sadie – who by then I had married – arranged for me to have shooting lessons. She thought it would be good for me to get away from the business. It actually brought in even more!

--- ooo ---

Socially, life was good, but I remember one embarrassing occasion when it almost caused me grief. Bury St Edmunds was very conservative with a small "c," but the local Young Conservatives decided to push things beyond the normal boundaries and arrange for a pyjama party to be held in a room above The One Bull – a pub on Angel Hill.

It was a wonderful evening but, somehow, the Bury Free Press – the local weekly paper – obtained a "team" photograph of those of us there. Tame by today's standards, it raised eyebrows among the older generation of the town.

On the day of its publication – a Friday – I went out with Freddie to value a country house somewhere in South Suffolk. We went around the property on our own, after which the lady of the house invited us into the kitchen for coffee. To my horror, there was a Bury Free Press with the photograph on the front page laid out on the table.

After a few minutes of general chat, she pointed to the paper and, in a shrill, upper-class voice, asked Freddie "Have you seen this? I really don't know what things are coming to!" Nothing was said at the time, but on the way back to the office in the car, Freddie asked simply, "Was it a good party then, Bedford?"

OUR REF.: JW/S.   ESTABLISHED 1866   YOUR REF.:

GEO. WRYCROFT & SONS
Partners: A. WRYCROFT, G. F. WRYCROFT, J. E. WRYCROFT

Builders and Contractors

ST. NEOTS - Huntingdonshire

Telegrams:
Wrycroft, Builders, St. Neots.

Telephone:
St. Neots 16

6th May 1943.

To whom this may concern.

This is to certify that Frederick John Bedford has been employed by us for 18 years – Eighteen Years – , he was apprenticed to us as a Carpenter & Joiner, Coffin Maker & Funeral Directors Assistant, & he is fully skilled in all branches of his trade.

Bedford has been in charge of works & a number of workmen & has also driven trucks & vehicles for some years past. He has had considerable experience in construction works, formwork for reinforced concrete, etc. He is most honest & reliable, & has been a most valued employee.

Signed.   *J.E.Wrycroft*

for & upon behalf of:-
Geo.Wrycroft & Sons .

THE SUPREME SACRIFICE

2 St. Neots Soldiers Killed

Two popular young men from the St. Neots district were last week reported to have been killed in action in the Central Mediterranean theatre. They were Pte. Fredk. John Bedford, of Eaton Socon, only son of Mr. and Mrs. J. Bedford, of Cambridge-st. (whose death was reported in our last issue and whose photograph is reproduced here) and Acting L/Bdr. Harry Sidney George Ranson R.F.A., son of Mrs. Nutcher, of 56, Russell-st.

Both men were 34 years of age. Pte. Bedford was married, with two young children, but L/Bdr. Ranson was single.

The latter had lived nearly all his life in St. Neots and before the war was employed by Mr. Fortescue, fishmonger, of High-st. He had been in the Army over three years, two of which had been spent overseas. He has three brothers serving in the Army—Fredk. in the R.A.O.C., Percy in the Suffolk Regt. and Charles in the Beds. and Herts. Regt.

L/Bdr. Ranson and Pte. Bedford, by a coincidence, were both keen members of St. Neots St. Mary's Football Club, the former having won two cups and medals whilst playing for that team.

Above: Dad's reference from George Wrycroft & Sons.

Top right: Dad with his tennis trophies.

Right: Dad, Mum, Mary and me.

Left: Press announcement, Dad killed in Italy.

Below: Cemetery at Cassino, with monastery on the mountain top.

Above: On my bike.

Above: Sadie with my first car.

Left: Visiting St Neots, Easter 1956 – Note no helmet!

Bottom left: Wedding Bells – St Faiths Church, King's Lynn, January 1961.

Below: Family Portrait 1971 – Paul, Sadie, Michael and James.

First advertisement in Lynn News and Advertiser, October 1966.

Grandad Bedford outside the Swaffham Office, 1966.

Left: Inside the Swaffham office with Pam Newman, secretary, 1967.

Right: New office headquarters at The Hollies, Swaffham, 1972.

Above: Rehearsing at Tom Ashton's house late 1950's. Trombone - Marcus Robb,
Trumpet - Alan Bland, Bass - Oswald Ashton, Clarinet - Dennis Sewell,
Banjo - an aspiring "Lonnie Donnegan".

Sadly Oswald and Dennis both died too young but recently I heard from Alan in New Zealand who
has requested a copy of the book!

Above: Agents being introduced to new technology at the Bury Free Press, 1982. Matthew
Fullerton, Me, Tim Dempsey, Clive Parkyn, Roger Davidson, Paul Bedford.

Chapter 6

Best of Both Worlds

I was thoroughly enjoying my job at Rutters. As I have said on many occasions since, if you are happy in your work, you will probably be good at it, and I think this was the case with me.

Socially, there was plenty going on in Bury but, most weekends, I would return on my motorcycle to King's Lynn. They say absence makes the heart grow stronger, and again that was the case with me.

By then, I was regularly playing hockey for Pelicans. On Saturdays after hockey, I would meet up with various friends then – usually after several pints of beer! – we would head for The Rose & Crown in Wisbech, where a dance was held that seemed to attract every eligible young person living in The Fens.

I don't think Sadie thought I was leading a celibate life in Bury and I encouraged her to go out in the week. Her occasional partners included John Wildbur, who was to become my accountant when I launched my own business, and William Landles, who was back at Blackfriars Chambers preparing to take the family business over from Collings. Sadly William, who I played hockey with at Pelicans, died in his fifties, but his sons, Tim and Simon, have continued to run the office and sale room.

Sadie appeared in several productions for the King's Lynn Operatic & Dramatic Society and had had several boyfriends. Before I left King's Lynn for Bury, we both appeared in a production of *Oklahoma*. Sadie was one of the can-can girls. As an estate agent, I was typecast as a cowboy!

Although I had met several girls in Bury who had become friends, none of these relationships had become "serious," so there was no reason why Sadie couldn't come down to Bury for the odd weekend. After work on Saturday, she would travel on the train to Ely where she would sit in state by the coal fire in the ladies' waiting room until I arrived to pick her up in a borrowed car – usually Peter Hart's.

It was during this period of our lives that we cemented many friendships, most of which have endured to this day. One of the results of my Norfolk and Suffolk lives overlapping was that as my Bury friends got to know Sadie, I had to be a bit more careful about my activities there during the week.

Looking back, some of the things we got up to were pretty irresponsible. I remember a firework party at Clare Country Club, which a crowd of us from Bury went to. Standing against the glow of the night sky, I spotted my pal George Langley wearing a duffle coat. For some reason or other, I decided it would be a good idea to lob a lit banger in his pocket. What I didn't realise was that he already had a pocketful of fireworks! Even today, I can remember him silhouetted against the night sky, struggling out of his coat and managing to get it at arm's length just before the explosion. As the smoke cleared, there stood George holding the charred remnants of his coat. He bellowed like a wounded bull and chased me round the grounds. Finally, Wendy, a girlfriend who had driven me to the Club, managed to lock me in a lavatory. Once she and friends had managed to calm George down, I talked to him through the locked door. I apologised profusely and suggested we should meet in The Angel Hotel the following morning, which we did. There, we arrived at a settlement. I gave George my duffel coat and £2 to make up for the fact that his was lined and mine wasn't. We shook hands and still remain good friends.

--- ooo ---

As our careers improved and we became a bit more affluent, the Angel Hotel became a regular meeting place.

In those days, if you entered up the steps and turned to the right in the hall, you came to a cocktail bar. Approached separately, but also at the front of the hotel, was the Pickwick Bar, which was for gentlemen only. The bar that separated them was manned by a wonderful "old-school" barmaid called Mabel. She was very discreet. I clearly remember an evening when I was on my own in the gents' bar and she came round the partition that separated it from the cocktail bar to inform me that "Sir may wish to know that Miss So-and-so is in the cocktail bar." I can't remember who it was – or whether I rushed round to the cocktail bar or beat a hasty retreat!

From five o'clock every Friday evening, local agents, solicitors and other professionals would congregate in the Pickwick Bar. Any problems that hadn't been sorted out during the week were usually settled then.

One thing I learnt then – something that served me well in bringing up my family – was that the sons of successful businessmen should not be given too much money without earning it. In my early days in Bury, when I was earning relatively little, a couple of individuals would flourish the large white £5 notes in circulation at the time when the rest of us were all contributing to a modest kitty. Both made a good job of messing up their lives!

Senior partners such as Freddie Laws and Michael Hall of local solicitors, Greene & Greene, met regularly for lunch in The Angel's dining room on a Wednesday, no doubt taking advantage of the opportunity to hatch up clever schemes to the benefit of their clients.

Freddie was certainly a bit of a showman. He drove a large Ford – usually a Zephyr – and for several years chose a convertible model, most likely to keep his two daughters happy. He was one of the first people I knew to have a personal number plate – DCF1. Bearing in mind his initials were FAL (Frederick Arthur Laws), this seemed a bit odd. One day, I plucked up courage to ask him what DCF stood for. Displaying his usual degree of modesty and a broad smile, he replied "Damn Clever Fellow!" That he was!

--- ooo ---

I have always loved jazz. To begin with, I shared the interest with my pals from school and St Neots – the Craig brothers and David Flint. When Louis Armstrong and his All Stars made their first tour of the UK, we made a pilgrimage to Olympia in London. This vast building wasn't an ideal venue for jazz musicians. Louis and the warm-up act, Humphrey Lyttleton and his band, performed on a raised circular stage that revolved quite slowly (fortunately!) and the acoustics were far from ideal. But we didn't notice any of that. Wedged up in "the gods" – we couldn't afford the expensive seats – we thought it was marvellous!

During my early years in Bury, The Carlton Hotel in Newmarket regularly had jazz events – often featuring two bands – and what was billed as an "all-nighter." I think they went on until about two or three o'clock in the morning. This was the time of the "trad" boom, so we were lucky to be entertained by the likes of Mick Mulligan and his vocalist, George Melly, Terry Lightfoot, Freddy Randle, Humphrey Lyttleton, Acker Bilk and my favourite, Chris Barber.

Many years later, when I was slightly more comfortably off, I was delighted to sponsor a Chris Barber concert at The Theatre Royal in Bury St Edmunds. Like most fans, I was a frustrated musician, but this was also the skiffle era, which gave non-musicians like me our opportunity. Several of us would occasionally "perform" together, with me playing either an improvised double bass made from a tea chest and broom handle or, occasionally, a washboard.

I was very friendly with Oswald Ashton, a young trainee solicitor whose father was Tom Ashton – the senior partner of Bankes Ashton, a Bury firm that has since become part of Ashton KCJ Solicitors. Oswald was a very competent musician and, along with Alan Bland, the local dentist's son, on trumpet and Dennis Sewell, a very good clarinettist, would perform at various parties. Desperate to join, I borrowed a banjo. Once I'd mastered a few chords, Oswald invited me to some practice sessions at his family's home in Horsecroft Road. These days, the house is owned by some friends of ours. I hear the echoes of those evenings in the late 1950s every time I'm there!

Typically, we would be invited to tea. Then, before going upstairs to practice, Oswald would tap on the sitting room door and we would all troop in to be introduced to his father. Tom – a marvellous man from a previous era who would still be wearing his wing-collar – would lower his copy of *The Times* and peer at us over his half-moon glasses. Addressing his father as "sir," Oswald would introduce each of us in turn. That done, we were free to enjoy the serious part of the evening.

The Swinging Sixties might have been just around the corner, but life at the Ashtons' was still a bit Victorian. At the time, Bankes Ashton had a main office on the corner of Guildhall and Abbeygate Streets and an overflow office in Guildhall Street, immediately opposite Rutters. In the days before sophisticated telephone systems, there was a lot of coming and going between the two offices. On weekdays, staff at Bankes Ashton wore sombre business suits. Some, such as Tom and his brother John, wore winged collars but, on Saturday mornings, everyone wore scruffy tweed jackets and cords. Dress down days are nothing new!

Some years later, when I came to acquire the lease of my own premises in Swaffham, Tom Ashton kindly not only gave me a reference but offered himself as a guarantor. Once I was installed, John Ashton, his wife and his children would troop into the office to say hello every summer en route to their annual holiday in Sheringham. I rather think Tom had asked them to call to check that I was still in business!

John died just a few years ago now, shortly after his 100th birthday party – an event Sadie and I were privileged to attend. We really enjoyed being on the "young" table!

--- ooo ---

In those days, we did our serious drinking at the local Conservative Club, but it closed at 10.30pm. So that we didn't have to bring the evening to a close, Peter Hart and I negotiated an arrangement with the doorman of a dance that alternated between Great Barton Village Hall and Culford Village Hall on Thursdays. He'd let us in for 2s 6d (12.5p) – half the regular entrance fee – on the promise that we wouldn't dance, at least not until the last dance. The attraction was the price of the beer, which was similar to that at the Con Club, and that it allowed us to carry on drinking until midnight.

On one occasion, I remember Neil Burman, a friend from King's Lynn, was sharing digs with me while he was working in Bury. When I mentioned a dance at Culford Village Hall, he said he would very much like to join me as he had been a boarder at Culford School nearby. Peter and I managed to get Neil in at the "mates" rate, after which we worked our way to the bar. Neil insisted on buying us a drink and moved to the front of the crowd. It was then that the lady behind the bar turned round. Both she and Neil were clearly surprised. Neil cried "Sally!!!" and she replied "Neil!!!" With her face blushing, the first thing she said was "I'm married now" – I have no idea why. It turned out that she had been a matron in Neil's boarding house in his days at the school!

--- ooo ---

It was during these happy bachelor years that I met Jeff Lawrence, who worked at the local builder's merchants, Marlows. His parents lived a few doors away from my digs in York Road. Jeff's father was manager of the local Woolworths store, a pillar of the local business community and, I believe, a stalwart of the local Rotary Club.

It soon became clear that Jeff had led a fairly sheltered life. Peter and I decided to fix this. One New Year's Eve, we invited him to join us and other friends at the Gentlemen's Bar at The Angel. When we got there, we sat Jeff on a bar stool, pointed to the top row of bottles, which comprised various liqueurs and other exotic drinks, and said that, on New Year's Eve, everyone was expected to start at one end of the row and see how far along the bar they could get. Jeff accepted the challenge! After the first three or four drinks, Peter and I quietly started to hang back. This was just as well: at the end of the evening, we had to carry Jeff out, put him in the back of Peter's car and drive him home!

At about ten o'clock the next morning, I took a call in the office from Mrs Lawrence, who was pretty upset and wanted to know what we had done to "her Jeffrey" as, apart from being violently ill all over the hall carpet, he had had a bladder malfunction in the bedroom and it had been very difficult to wake him up in the morning. Lying, I told her that we had tried to control his drinking, but I don't think she believed me. About half an hour later, Mr Lawrence telephoned and apologised for his wife's outburst, saying he understood that "boys would be boys." Jeff remains a good friend and, indeed, was best man at our wedding.

These were just some of the friendships made in my early days in Bury that have endured throughout my life. Others I met back then included young solicitors, Donald Clarke, John Sheerin and Jos Bird; Bernard Huffey, a flamboyant car salesman; and Sandy Hills, who was in the corn trade. Some are sadly no longer with us, but the memories remain.

--- ooo ---

While I was enjoying my job and the social life in Bury, Sadie was getting a bit fed-up. This was understandable: at times, I was only going back to King's Lynn every other weekend. I had to make up my mind whether or not we had a future together.

Peter had a regular girlfriend and, occasionally, I would go out with her sister. One Friday, just before I left for King's Lynn, Peter said he would probably be coming up to Norfolk over the weekend and suggested that we all meet up for a drink in The Globe Hotel, King's Lynn, on the Sunday evening.

My Sunday night farewells with Sadie were getting increasingly difficult but, on this occasion, I persuaded her that I needed to get back to Bury earlier than usual and left her parents' home at about 7.30pm. On entering the bar at The Globe Hotel, I found Peter there with both the sisters. I felt distinctly uncomfortable about this, but decided to have a drink before making my excuses and leaving. I had it all lined up – "It will take me an hour to get back to Bury on my motorbike, so I have to get away" – but just before I finished my pint, disaster struck. I knew that Sadie's parents would often go for a drink with another couple on a Sunday evening, but I had never known them to visit The Globe. I have to say that Sadie's mother, Lettie, and I never got along terribly well. I think she had deep suspicions of my activities in Bury. Well, now she had all the ammunition she needed! She immediately dragged her husband, Ray, from the bar and disappeared. A few minutes later, I set out on what seemed like my longest-ever journey from King's Lynn to Bury St Edmunds.

After this episode, I had to mend fences with Sadie. She wasn't sure my intentions were still honourable. We patched things up, but I knew decision time was approaching fast. On Christmas Eve 1959, I returned to King's Lynn, wondering what I should buy Sadie for Christmas. I went to the local record shop, Wheelers, and bought a Frank Sinatra LP but, in view of recent events, I thought I needed to do a bit better than this. On an impulse, I strolled to Bird & Varney, the Ford garage in Railway Road where Sadie's father, Ray, was a partner. Catching him alone in the small kiosk on the forecourt where they served petrol, I explained that I wanted to get engaged to Sadie. Puffing my chest out, I said that I was now on £500 a year and had excellent prospects. He said he was delighted and that I should visit them at home that evening for a drink.

By this time, Sadie was working at a different hairdresser's in Blackfriars Street so, on what I imagine was the busiest afternoon of their year, it was there that I went next. Whispering in the owner's ear, I explained the mission I was on. Thankfully, he understood. Halfway through some poor lady's appointment, he told Sadie to put her coat on as she had to go out with me for 15 minutes.

By this time, I had graduated from a motorbike to a van. I bundled Sadie in, drove up New Conduit Street, turned right into High Street and stopped outside Speeds, the jewellers. It was there that I explained to a somewhat bemused Sadie that I wanted to buy her a Christmas present – a ring. We went inside and asked to see some engagement rings. After trying on a couple, Sadie said she would like a particular one. She has since confessed that, after going out with me for four or five years, she wasn't going to make a fuss over a ring at that stage. She then rushed back to the hairdressers. The ladies who had been sitting disgruntled under dryers were immediately happy when she explained where she had been.

The evening at Sadie's home – 240 Wootton Road, King's Lynn – was not a bundle of fun. By the time we got there, Ray was obviously in serious trouble with Lettie for having agreed to an engagement without talking to her first. Peace broke out when after a certain amount of interrogation, we said we wouldn't get married for "at least a year."

Chapter 7

Gage Cottage

As luck would have it, what was described as "a quaint and attractive semi-detached period cottage" in Hengrave, a very pretty estate village about three miles out of Bury St Edmunds, came onto the market just a few weeks after we got engaged.

The details, of which I still have a copy, said that it was "of typical Suffolk construction: timber framing, lath and plaster under a wired thatched roof" and that the accommodation was "worthy of improvement by installing modern conveniences." The sale particulars, which were "believed to be correct, but their accuracy is not guaranteed," revealed that, outside, it had a timber stall and pail closet. They were right – it did need improvement! But the price was good – just £900 for the freehold – and the rateable value was just £5, which meant the current half-year rates were just £2 2s 1d (about £2.10). Water rates added one more pound.

That weekend, I went back to Norfolk and told Sadie I thought it would be an ideal first home. I had checked with my mother that I could cash the £50 Premium Bond and I discovered that Sadie also had about £50 in savings. Bearing in mind our promise not to get married until the following year, Lettie couldn't see any point in us buying a house at this stage. But, in the end, she and Ray were persuaded to drive Sadie down on the Sunday afternoon and take a look at the house.

Sadie's parents lived in an immaculate semi-detached house in the suburbs of King's Lynn. Seeing the property I had in mind as our first home, Lettie was horrified at the idea that her daughter should live in what she described as a "Suffolk Mud Hut." I tried to explain the potential I saw in the property, but to no avail. They returned to Norfolk with a very tearful Sadie in the back of their car.

Undeterred, I set about working out how I could purchase the property. No building society would touch it in its present state, but the local authority, Thingoe District Council, had a scheme to grant mortgages on "for improvement" properties when finance could not be obtained elsewhere. The council's surveyor was Sam Casson. His son, John, still practices as a surveyor in Bury. Sam and I had met a few times on business, so I took him out to Hengrave to see what I had in mind. After looking around, he asked "how much of the £900 do you need to borrow?" I looked him in the eye and said "£800." There was a slight intake of breath, but he said he thought that would be okay.

The following weekend, I persuaded Sadie to part with her £50 of savings. Still nervous about the mortgage, I managed to talk the vendors into selling the cottage for £800. On 12 February 1960, I paid the deposit – £80 – and telephoned Sam to ask how the mortgage application was progressing. He said the council's finance committee was a bit nervous but, when I told him I was buying the cottage for £100 less than the asking price and only wanted to borrow 90 percent of that – £720 – he said he was pretty sure it would be agreed.

Suitably assured, I contacted Michael Baker, a young solicitor and one of my drinking pals, and asked if his firm, Woolnough Gross, Son & Chamberlain, would act for me. Contracts were duly exchanged and completion took place on 10 March 1960. The legal fees amounted to £23 1s 0d (£23.05) or about 2.8 percent of the purchase price – and they were supposed to be doing me a favour!

I drew up the plans for the modernisation myself and submitted them to the council. They were approved very quickly by today's standards.

My pal, Jeff Lawrence, who was employed by Marlows, the builders' merchants, produced a schedule of costs with the help of one or two of his mates in the building trade, and an estimate of £202 11s 4d (£202.56) was arrived at for the work. In addition, I had had an estimate from L V Avis, a local thatcher, for the repair of the roof. Including the ridge, that came to £49 10s 0d (£49.50), with an additional £9 10s 0d (£9.50) for the wire netting to cover the ridge and the gable. I couldn't afford the extra £22 it would have cost to cover the whole roof with netting.

This was all fine, but I had no money. With fingers crossed, I approached Freddie Laws, who kindly said he would lend me up to £300. I also applied to Thingoe District Council, who agreed to make a grant of £101 2s 5d (£101.12), to be paid when the work was completed. The cheque was posted to me on 29 December 1960.

From the spring until the end of the year, I spent every evening and weekend at the cottage. Jeff, who was to become my best man, and I were the labourers. Peter Abbot, a local plumber, and a few other tradesmen, helped as well.

I vividly remember one summer's evening. Jeff and I were merrily swinging a sledge hammer, knocking a wall out, when a couple of local architects, Mike Heaton and Alan Swales, pulled up to see how we were getting on. They told us to stop work immediately. If the next stud had been removed, they thought the house would have collapsed. A support was urgently required!

In those days, there weren't such things as reclaimed building material suppliers. Instead, I found a railway sleeper and installed it in what was to be the access between the sitting room and the dining room.

Some 50 years later, I called at the cottage and introduced myself. The owners showed me around the ground floor. They were very proud to be living in such an "old" cottage. I couldn't help but smile. When they asked why, I told them that the main beam they were so proud of was, in fact, a railway sleeper!

My records show that I obtained a further advance of £250 from the council in December 1960 which, together with the payment of the grant, enabled me to pay Freddie Laws back and buy some furniture in time for us to move in following our marriage. The date for the wedding had been fixed as Saturday 14 January 1961 – just over the year we had promised Sadie's mother that we would wait.

During the frantic months completing the renovation of the cottage, we had no time to think of a name for it. Just before Christmas, I was explaining the problem to Peter and he immediately said "It's obvious! You must call it Gage Cottage."

"Why is that?" I asked. He explained that Hengrave Hall and the estate around it on which the cottage stood had originally belonged to one Sir Thomas Gage – the man who introduced the greengage tree to Britain. I thanked him and duly asked the firm's sign writer to prepare a board, which I erected at the front door.

--- ooo ---

A few weeks before our wedding day, it dawned on me that we needed to furnish the cottage.

I had just changed my car for the first Mini van that Botwoods sold in Bury St Edmunds. According to the brochure, it was "burnt orange" and I still remember the number – PCF 501.

Sadie and I managed to take a few days off work together to set off in search of the things we needed. One day, we attended four or five different furniture sales, including one at my old stomping ground – Blackfriars Hall – another at a country house near Narborough, one in Rickinghall and, finally, one at T W Gaze in Diss. I don't remember being that choosy at the time, but we clearly bought well. Some of the things we bought that day are still in our home 50 years later!

Conveniently, Sadie and I had got engaged just before her 21st birthday[2]. A lot of the presents she got that year were things for her bottom drawer – fish knives and forks and other household items – so we had a lot of the small items we needed for our new home.

---

[2] She says I never actually asked her to marry me – just "would you like a ring?"

The one thing I can't remember buying was a bed. I think we got that second-hand from Sadie's parents.

--- ooo ---

As the wedding day approached, I had done nothing about a honeymoon other than vaguely suggest to Sadie that we should go to London to see a show.

The wedding was held at St Faith's Church in Gaywood, King's Lynn. As I mentioned, Jeff Lawrence was my best man, our respective sisters, Mary and Jane, were bridesmaids, and the ushers were six of my best pals from Pelicans: David Pugh, Richard Pugh, Neville Carter, Martin Gethin, John Wildbur and Ray Burn. The reception was held in The Duke's Head Hotel in King's Lynn.

Unlike our children's generation, who seem not to get married before their early thirties, Sadie and I were quite young – just 21 and 23, respectively.

Back then, it was quite usual for the majority of the guests to be friends of the bride and groom's parents, and this was true for us. Only a few of our mates were present – mainly members of Pelicans Hockey Club. Everything went well until about half-way through the meal, when about eight of them stood up and left the dining room. They had a most important fixture against Norwich Grasshoppers at North Runcton that afternoon! Sadie's mother was not amused.

It was then that I realised that Granny Baxter from St Neots, of whom I was very fond, was not at the wedding. Aunt Nessie, who by this time was living with her mother and looking after her, told me she was "not too well" but sent her best wishes.

Eventually, the time came for us to "escape" from King's Lynn. I had taken elaborate precautions. In those days, the groom's vehicle would typically be doctored in some way. Kippers would be tied to the exhaust pipe, most of the petrol would be drained from the tank or some other such prank would be perpetrated on the happy couple.

When John and Joy Wildbur had got married the year before, my friends and I came up with a cunning plan that John blamed solely on me. After his wedding, we were all invited to his parents' house. Foolishly, he telephoned his mother to say he had arrived safely. I was able to check the telephone number, which turned out to be one near Mildenhall that I recognised immediately. Peter Hart and I had carried out a stock take of the premises concerned – The Bull at Barton Mills. Armed with this intelligence, two car-loads of us excused ourselves from the Wilburs' and set off for Barton Mills. We arrived about ten o'clock, in time for a pint in the bar. When John walked in, we all froze but he didn't spot us at the far end of the bar. After picking up his pint, he retired to the honeymoon suite.

By then, Martin Gethin had located Joy's unlocked car in the courtyard. At the time, there was a malicious rumour that John had married Joy for the car – an Austin A35. He had only got a Ford Popular! Anyway, Martin was able to loosen the radiator cap, pour in some rice and then loosely replace the cap without tightening it. The following morning, John and Joy set out for Heathrow Airport but, halfway across Newmarket Heath, the car overheated. John got out, raised the bonnet and was confronted with a huge rice pudding! They had to be towed into Newmarket before they could complete their journey.

Because of this, I knew I needed to leave King's Lynn without John Wildbur following. We left The Duke's Head in one of the wedding cars, drove a couple of hundred yards, closely followed by John, and pulled up outside Marks & Spencer, where Sadie and I got out. John must have thought we'd gone shopping, but we walked through the store to its Norfolk Street entrance, where I had arranged for our Mini van to be parked. Norfolk Street was one way, so John couldn't turn left to follow us. As we left King's Lynn without him and headed across The Fens, I told Sadie I would like to spend the night somewhere near my home town, St Neots, so we could go and see Granny. Sadie immediately said she would like to give her her wedding bouquet.

Arriving at The George at Buckden, which was then on the A1 Great North Road, I parked the car, removed my tie and strolled nonchalantly up to the reception to ask if they had a room. The man behind the desk said "Of course, sir," so I said I would go and collect my wife and luggage. By then, the receptionist had twigged that we were honeymooners, so we were led up the staircase, along a corridor that seemed to be about 40 yards long, right down an even longer corridor and into the biggest bedroom I had ever seen. The only downside was that it had two twin beds. There was nothing for it other than to own up. "Have you got a room with a double bed?" I asked. "We're on our honeymoon." "Oh, you should have explained," he replied, "I'll take you to The Turpin Suite." I later discovered that it was named after Dick Turpin, the highwayman, who had been a regular visitor at The George in his time.

I think this receptionist must have been the only member of staff on duty as he turned out to be barman and waiter as well. Judging by how long it took our meal to arrive, he might even have been the cook!

The next morning, we drove the few miles to St Neots to Granny Baxter's house – the one opposite the golf club where I had stayed in my youth. When we walked in, I knew from the looks on Auntie Nessie's and her husband's faces that there was a problem. They confirmed the worst. Granny had died the day before – on our wedding day. They hadn't told us because they didn't want to spoil our big day.

I hadn't booked a hotel or theatre in London so, having heard the news, we decided to drive back to Hengrave and get on with sorting out our new home. A few days later, Sadie and I attended what, for both of us, was our first funeral. The next day, we made a day trip to London to see the original version of Lionel Bart's show, *Oliver.*

Chapter 8

Early Days at Hengrave

The early years of our marriage were very happy.

Peter Hart had married Ann Stamper, a farmer's daughter from Bardwell, about a year before we tied the knot. As well as working together, we saw a fair amount of one another socially.

Freddie Laws and his wife, Olive, had been very kind to me when I was a bachelor, frequently inviting me to supper at their house, Lilliput. This continued after we were married.

And I was enjoying work. Rutters' business was flourishing, Peter had become a partner and, although I never had the title, I was effectively the manager of residential house sales. More importantly, I was on commission, so things were improving financially.

That was important to me. Back then, wives of professional men weren't expected to work – one income would provide a reasonable living. It now seems bizarre, but some women were even forced to quit their jobs when they got married. These days, most wives work – some are the principal breadwinners. But there are exceptions, of course, and they don't always turn out well. A combination of not working and too much opportunity to indulge in retail "therapy" can lead to the collapse of otherwise sound marriages.

Having grown up to believe that the man's job in a marriage was to be the breadwinner, I never really wanted Sadie to go out to work, but there was no denying that, as a hairdresser, she could contribute quite a lot to our family's finances.

Our cottage at Hengrave was opposite the Hall, which was a girls' boarding school. Sadie went there regularly to cut the girls' hair. Olive Laws, one of her regular clients, sent along other friends. That was good but, one day when I came home, Sadie told me that Olive had introduced her to someone who lived in Stonebridge Avenue. "What's her name?" I asked. I can't remember her name, but I do remember she was the wife of a tax inspector!

--- ooo ---

In the early 1960s, Bury St Edmunds was a bustling town with a thriving weekly cattle market. On a Wednesday, the town would be full of farmers and lorries transporting cattle, sheep and pigs.

The firm most involved in this trade was Lacy Scott. At the time, it didn't seem very interested in selling houses. Unlike Rutters, it still thrives to this day, even without the cattle market, which has been turned into a shopping precinct called The Arc.

In the spring of 1962, just over a year after Sadie and I were married, a couple from Essex came into the office looking for a cottage to move to when they retired. As usual, I asked them for more details. What I didn't expect was for them to describe what, to all intents and purposes, was my house – Gage Cottage!

That evening I told Sadie about the couple and their interest. Hoping to start a family, she was reluctant to consider a move. I pointed out that the couple didn't seem to be in a hurry, which cheered her up a bit. When they returned to the office a few days later, I said I knew of a property that wasn't on the market, but could possibly be available by the time they wanted to move. They insisted on having a look.

The couple quite clearly loved Gage Cottage, and I promised to get back to them once I had discussed the possibility of selling it to them with my wife. They said that, if it would help, they could wait up to a year before moving in. I convinced Sadie it was a wonderful opportunity and said I would ask for £2,750 – more than twice what the property had cost us just a year before – with a 12-month completion date. They immediately agreed.

At the time, a year seemed an awfully long way off. They had a survey carried out, solicitors were instructed and I immediately started looking for our next home. Although I didn't let on to Sadie, there was really nothing I felt was suitable. When the time came for contracts to be exchanged, I played for time. I managed to persuade the purchasers that completion should be 12 months from exchange of contracts, not when we agreed the deal. That gave us until the following August. That autumn, Sadie went to the doctor's. When she came home, she confirmed she was pregnant.

--- ooo ---

I played for Pelicans for a while after moving to Bury but, eventually, I moved to Bury St Edmunds Hockey Club. This became the centre of our social world. Most of our friends were members: Robert and Judy Long, Ben and Jo Robins, Mick and Paddy Reed, and Harold and Jill Crystal, together with a local vet,

Chris, and his wife, Madeline Tew. They were all far more comfortably off than we were, but they made us most welcome. I particularly remember the regular get-togethers for drinks and a meal in The Vaults below The Angel Hotel.

That winter, I took a fair amount of stick from my friends over the fact that my wife, pregnant with our first child, had "nowhere to live." By the spring of 1963, with Sadie growing ever larger, I was beginning to get a bit desperate. There weren't many properties on the market that appealed to us, and the offers we had made on the ones that did hadn't been accepted.

One of my duties at Rutters was to look after the Mildenhall office on Tuesdays and Fridays. Every Friday lunchtime, I would have a drink and a sandwich in The Bell Hotel, where one of the regulars was Bill Cocksedge, a local builder. Talking to him one day, he mentioned that he was building eight bungalows at Burthorpe Green in Barrow, between Bury St Edmunds and Newmarket. He had sold several, but wondered if I would be interested in selling the rest. He gave me the plans and, at the weekend, I went to have a look at the site.

I suppose I was already a bit of a property snob, but I thought Plot 8, at the top of the hill, could be improved and that it would do the Bedford family as a stopgap. I am ashamed to confess that the improvements included adding stone facing to the brickwork around the front door!

I agreed to buy the property, which I called The Drum. This was the phrase Peter and I used to describe "ordinary" properties, in much the same way that motor dealers would sometimes refer to vehicles as "bangers."

The other events I remember clearly from 1963 were sitting with Sadie watching our very small black-and-white TV at the time of the Cuban Missile Crisis and discussing whether we were doing the right thing, bringing a child into the world. In the 50 years since then, I'm sure thousands of soon-to-be parents have had very similar conversations.

Paul was born on 31 July and we moved into our new bungalow a few weeks later. In November of that year, Sadie was in the kitchen cooking supper. She and I were, I think, watching the same television when the programme was interrupted to announce that President Kennedy had been shot. The question is often asked but, yes, we do remember where we were at that time!

The Drum might not have been an exciting property, but it was a perfectly comfortable home. While living there, we made friendships that have lasted all our lives. Acquaintances from the time include David Evans, a fruit farmer, and his wife Jean, who lived across the road. We also cemented our relationship with Ben and Jo Robins, who farmed just down the road at Denham.

But our stay at The Drum was to be a short one. We hadn't been there long when a building plot came up for sale in Hengrave, almost next door to Gage Cottage. We had always wanted to build our own house, so I decided to buy it. I was now earning a decent salary, so I had taken out a bigger mortgage than I had planned. After buying the bungalow, I had just a few hundred pounds left in the bank.

I instructed a local architect, Dick Warren, to draw up some plans, but there was a problem. Following a recession, a boom in the property market meant that building materials were in short supply. Bricks were particularly hard to come by. Many had to be imported from Belgium at the time.

Dick suggested we should design a house using the minimum number of bricks. He came up with a clever plan where the plinth would be in brickwork, the ground floor would be built in blocks and rendered, and the whole of the first floor would be what's properly called a Mansard roof, but often described as "Dutch." Constructed in timber, it would be hung with tiles.

At about this time, I received a telephone call from Robert Arnold, a partner in Cheffins, an auctioneer and estate agent with offices in Cambridge and Saffron Walden. Saying he had a proposition to put to me, he invited me to meet him in Saffron Walden. He, his partner, Paul Gooderham, and I spent a very convivial evening in a pub there, during which it emerged that they were planning to open an office in Newmarket. They wanted me to run it. I was very tempted. Sadie and I had several sleepless nights discussing the offer but, in the end, I decided to turn it down. This was mainly out of loyalty to Freddie and Peter, to whom I owed so much. Loyalty meant quite a lot back then, so I felt I had to tell Freddie. While I was immediately given a rise, this was not my sole motive for confiding in him.

Robert and Paul understood and respected my decision. They appointed Paul Goodman to manage their Newmarket office and, over the years, I got to know him well. I still tease him that he was "second choice"! Many years later, his daughter Charlotte came to work at Bedfords' Bury Office and became a very successful negotiator. Paul Gooderham and I remained both successful negotiator. Paul Gooderham and I remained both competitors and good friends for many years but, sadly, he died just a few years ago. He was an excellent businessman and a wonderful human being. I was proud to be among a congregation of nearly 600 at his funeral in Saffron Walden.

--- ooo ---

The council approved the plans for the new house at Hengrave, but the only way we could afford to build it was to sell The Drum and move into rented accommodation, so that's what we did.

The three of us – Sadie, our son, Paul, and I – moved into Camilla, a bungalow in Great Barton Park. My wife was a great fan of Princess Diana and still gets very irritated when I remind her that we lived in "Camilla's" bungalow!

Like most marriages, we have had our ups and downs, and one of the downs was when we were in this rented property. There was the stress of dealing with the builders working on the new house: we seemed to rub one and other up the wrong way! It sounds stupid, but Camilla was a badly planned bungalow. One or two doors opened the wrong way and, if it had been our own property, we would soon have sorted it out. But we survived this period of our lives. The house at Hengrave was completed – we called it Gage House – and the three of us moved in.

At the time we married, my sister had warned Sadie that she should only have furniture that was fitted with wheels. How right she was! Paul had lived in four properties by the time he was two years old.

We had not been in the new house very long when something happened that was to change the whole course of my career. Freddie had a minor health scare and, with just two daughters and no son, became concerned about the future of the firm. It was he who managed the side of the business that dealt with landowners and estates – not just in Suffolk and Norfolk, but as far afield as Nottinghamshire. He knew he could trust Peter and me with the estate agency side of the business, which was developing very successfully, but the only help he had was from one or two land-agent assistants who were a bit short in the "chin" department. He didn't think they could handle the business on their own.

Unbeknown either to myself or, I believe, to Peter, Freddie had been having meetings with potential suitors. One rather dull Friday afternoon, I remember being summoned to a meeting, along with the rest of the staff, to be told that a merger had been agreed with Smiths Gore. The new firm would be called Rutters Smiths Gore.

A few days later, a couple of Smiths Gore's partners came in and interviewed us one by one. Smiths Gore was a formidable firm of national land agents that, back then, had offices in Peterborough, York and other similar regional centres. They acted for some of the largest property owners in the country, including The Church Commissioners, but I wasn't quite sure what they knew about selling houses in Bury St Edmunds.

The name of the partner who interviewed me escapes me, but I am sure it was hyphenated. I imagine he had a few thousand acres as well. He understood that, while I was "unqualified," I was "quite a good estate agent," saying the latter in a way that gave me the clear impression that he carried a mouthwash in his briefcase to use every time he uttered the words "estate agent." At the end of the meeting, he told me that, in the next financial year, I would earn an additional £50 a year. I thanked him, but left the room with a heavy heart.

There weren't many changes to start with, but the plan was clearly to expand the land agency side of the business. That duly happened. New staff were recruited, which increased the demands on the office space available. One of the firm's clients owned a small tobacconist shop immediately opposite Rutters' office at 86 Guildhall Street. It was run by a lady of indeterminate years who was a heavy smoker. She was always referred to as "smelly Annie," so I imagine Annie was her name. Whatever, the end of her lease was approaching, so Peter and I suggested to the partners that her shop would make an ideal stand-alone sales office for the estate agency side of the business. Approaches were made to the planning office, but we didn't think the council would have any objections. Virtually every other property in the street was being used for offices. The owner was sympathetic to granting the firm a new lease, so plans and costings were drawn up. I was very excited about the prospect of virtually running my own office under the Rutters' banner, so you can imagine my disappointment when, at the following partners' meeting, it was decided not to proceed. We would have to make do with the limited accommodation at Number 86.

--- ooo ---

Having started to think about having an office of my own, this
became an increasing feature of my thoughts. Sadie was pregnant
again and, together with Paul, we would regularly visit parents
and in-laws in King's Lynn at the weekends. While there, I would
often read the local paper and, out of professional interest, take a
stroll round the town looking in the agents' windows. The way
agents in Norfolk did business was several light years short of the
standard we had set in Bury St Edmunds, and I increasingly
became convinced there was an opening. My confidence had been
boosted by the approach from Cheffins, who were clearly sure I
could run an office on my own, and I was well aware of the value
of the fees Rutters was earning in Mildenhall, the office I manned
for just two days a week!

James, our second son, was born in April 1966 and, at about
that time, Sadie said she was prepared to support my ambition of
starting my own business. Her buy-in was very important. We had
a very comfortable lifestyle in a nice house just outside Bury St
Edmunds, but the only money we had was tied up in that
property. While I didn't have a business plan, I thought that, if we
could get a good price for Gage House, we would have enough to
buy a modest property in Norfolk and two or three thousand
pounds to help me get a new business started.

Out of loyalty to Freddie and Peter, I told them that I planned
to move to Norfolk before the end of the year. I was giving them
six months' notice. The fact that I was open with them – and going
far enough away not to mess on their doorstep – suited us all, so I
continued to work for Rutters, earning good money while taking a

day of holiday now and then to make exploratory trips into Norfolk.

Chapter 9

Why Swaffham?

From time to time, I would help out at Rutters' office in Thetford.

One day, Peter asked me to go and value a bungalow in Swaffham, a town that, other than on my way from King's Lynn to Norwich, I don't think I had ever visited before. I arrived in good time to visit local agents to get an idea of the prices of comparable properties. To my amazement, there was only one firm in the town – a firm called Noel Abel that appeared to open only on Tuesdays and Thursdays, and then only if the owner felt like it!

After the appointment, I took a drive around the town. I was pleasantly surprised at the number of relatively new estates there and the number of retirement bungalows. The other thing that struck me was the number of different agents' boards I saw. Firms from Downham Market, King's Lynn, Fakenham, Dereham, Watton and the odd one from Thetford were all represented. It suddenly hit me between the eyes that no one firm dominated. There was clearly an opening in Swaffham. Up to then, I had been looking for business premises to rent in King's Lynn, so I clearly had a decision to make.

My good friend Martin Gethin, who had been an usher at our wedding, was a solicitor in King's Lynn with Pounder, Brown & Gethin. As with William Landles, his father had died young. I decided that, when the time came, I would talk to Martin and ask him to act for me. Sadly, one weekend at Hengrave – it was in the autumn of 1965 – I received a telephone call from my sister to say that Martin and another sailor were missing, believed drowned at Brancaster. The next day, it was confirmed – the bodies had been recovered. I attended Martin's funeral at St Margaret's, King's Lynn. After the service, I talked to his brother, John, and confided in him that I had ideas about setting up on my own one day in Norfolk. John said that, if I did want to pursue it, he would be happy to give any advice, and that I should not hesitate to contact him.

--- 000 ---

After my visit to Swaffham, I thought this was the moment I should talk to someone "independent" about my ideas and take some advice. I told John both what I had been thinking about for King's Lynn and how tempted I was to open in Swaffham. He thought King's Lynn offered better prospects – it was a large market town with rapidly expanding new industries – but he also understood the appeal of Swaffham, where there was virtually no competition.

After a further week or two of visits to Swaffham, including one weekend when I took Sadie, we decided to move to Swaffham and open an office there. Not only did it look like a great opportunity, there were financial considerations to take into account. It was cheaper to buy a house in Swaffham, and offices there were likely to be cheaper to rent than in King's Lynn. Another bonus, given the circle of friends we had built up in the first five years of our marriage, all of whom lived in or around

Bury St Edmunds, was that it was a lot quicker to travel to Bury from Swaffham than from King's Lynn. Although inspired by the thought of starting a new business, we were apprehensive about leaving Suffolk.

We placed Gage House on the market at a rather optimistic £8,250 and, very quickly, I found premises at 95 Market Place, Swaffham, that I thought ideal. I can't remember the exact terms, but the property was in pretty poor order and I know the rent was much-reduced for the first couple of years as I was required to spend quite a lot of money to bring it up to scratch.

For some years, Rutters had acted for Bennetts, a builder of retirement bungalows. While they mainly sold the properties they built themselves, they instructed us when it came to some of the more difficult-to-sell plots. Josh Bennett had started the firm just after the war. It used a local architect in Lakenheath – a chap called John Whisson. Knowing something about him, I arranged to meet John at Swaffham and asked him to draw up plans for alterations to the offices and a new shop front. I still have a copy of the plan, dated 14 June 1966. The plans must have been passed very quickly as there was a lot of building work to be completed before I opened the office, which was on 7 October 1966. John obviously had a rapport with the local council as Bennetts were developing one or two sites in the town, and that must have helped.

Gage House had been on the market for some time – long enough to make me nervous about how I was going to be able to buy a house and finish off the office. I had dealt with the Midland Bank since I had started saving. I remember going to the St Neots branch with my mother to open an account. Based on this, I persuaded the manager of the Bury St Edmunds branch to assure his colleague in King's Lynn that I was a worthwhile customer, and that my application for a loan should be approved. My business plan was very much on the "back of an envelope," but he agreed to lend me up to £1,000, which enabled me to crack on with the office work.

Equally concerning was that we were finding it difficult to find a suitable property in Swaffham. Then, in July, I saw a Dereham agent's board on a house in Mangate Street, a few doors away from the town's George Hotel. The three-storey terraced house fronted onto what then was the main A47 King's Lynn to Norwich road, which ran through the centre of Swaffham. The property was being offered for £2,500, but I managed get it for £2,200 on the basis that I was a "cash" purchaser. At the time we shook hands, I was far from sure where the cash would come from, but I hoped to have it very shortly. A young dentist and his wife had viewed Gage House a couple times, so I made contact with them. The dentist said that, while he would like to buy the house, he couldn't afford the asking price. He offered £7,500 instead.

After a bit of haggling, I agreed the sale at £7,600. That was on 3 August 1966 – not long before the date we agreed for completion. The sale summary I still have said that would be on or before 7 October 1966.

Fortunately, contracts were exchanged fairly quickly, which enabled me to complete the purchase of the Swaffham house. I had an outstanding mortgage with the Leeds Permanent Building

Society of £2,600, which meant that, together with the few hundred pounds savings we had in the bank, we would have a total of £5,000 to buy the property in Swaffham and start the business. I told Sadie that I intended paying cash for the Swaffham house, honouring my rash promise at the time the sale was agreed, and that I would use the other £3,000 to start the business. I assured her that I wouldn't risk more than £3,000 so that, if things didn't work out, we would at least have a roof over our heads.

--- ooo ---

On our regular trips to Swaffham, Paul, who was just three years old at the time, had great difficulty in pronouncing the name of the town. It always came out "Foffum." And so it was that we came to call our new home there Foffum House. On Sunday evenings, there was always a tail-back of traffic from the lights in Swaffham – mainly returning day-trippers from Yarmouth – and it was amusing to see people in the cars stationary outside our house reading the name, then breaking into a smile when the penny dropped!

During our early years of marriage, holidays consisted of a week in King's Lynn, with either my parents or Sadie's, and days out in Hunstanton or at Sadie's parents' beach hut in Snettisham. One trip that sticks in my mind is that we made early in June 1963 – it might even have been over the May Bank Holiday weekend. We were with my parents and I had the week off. On the Sunday, I told Sadie I fancied going to Scotland. Sadie was about seven months pregnant with Paul at the time. My "wheels" had graduated to a second-hand Triumph Herald Convertible so, despite a lot of pressure from the grannies-to-be, we set off. We drove all the way to Edinburgh that day, arriving early in the evening. I drove into Princes Street and parked – yes, parked! – by the doorway of a hotel. The entrance was sandwiched between two shops and the hotel was on the floor above.

We booked in for the night. The weather was marvellous so, the next day, we set off for the west coast. We had a wonderful few days there, with the hood down on the car and our first "baby" – a Sheltie collie called Susie – on the back seat with her nose permanently in the air.

The day before we headed home, we went to Oban, where there was much excitement as the Prime Minister, Harold Macmillan, was holidaying nearby on the Isle of Mull and was due to return to London that day, having had to cut his holiday short. Before heading home, we decided to stay one last night, and booked into a hotel at Crianlarich. The following morning, as we came down to breakfast, we saw a newspaper with a very large headline about the Profumo affair sitting on a table in the hall. "So that's why the Prime Minister had to cut his holiday short," we thought!

--- ooo ---

But back to 1966...

If I was to start a new business, it was clear it might be quite a long time before we had another proper holiday. So, in July, we booked a ten-day break in Ibiza which, back then, was a nice quiet Mediterranean island. Its reputation for discos and drug taking came much later.

We hadn't been abroad before – few Britons had – but pictures in various magazines suggested we needed to dress properly. To get ourselves equipped, we took a half-day off and went to Cambridge. I bought a lightweight suit from Bodgers, one of the city's principal gentlemen's outfitters, and Sadie bought what I believe is called a coat dress.

In those days, when you got off the plane, there would be a photographer recording the event. A photograph shows us and other passengers dressed in suits and ties as if we were going to a Buckingham Palace Garden Party! Fifty years later, when returning from Italy on a Ryanair flight, I was tempted to contact *The Guinness Book of Records* to tell them there were four of us on the plane wearing jackets!

Looking at my diary for the year, I see that I had just over two weeks' holiday in all – the remainder being spent organising the office in Swaffham. However, from the day I returned until Friday 30 September, when I left Rutters, there was hardly a minute when I didn't have an appointment. Indeed, on the very last day, I visited a property south of Bury and another in Mildenhall. At the end of the afternoon, I shook hands with Peter and Freddie with a lump in my throat. While they were sorry to see me go, Peter, in particular, understood. I was 29 years old. If I was ever going to take the plunge, it had to be then.

Having said my farewells on the Friday, I travelled to Swaffham on Monday 3 October 1966, hoping that the secretary I had interviewed a couple of weeks before would turn up. She arrived when we had agreed – at 10 am – and promptly set about sorting out the office, setting up filing systems and so on.

The previous week, I had erected a board in the window announcing my intention to open. This generated two letters and a telephone call, so I had three invitations to view properties to get me started. The first was Point House in Great Dunham, which I visited on the Monday afternoon. The vendor clearly liked my pitch and asked me to offer it for sale at £1,250. I was off to a flying start!

I had also been asked by Bennetts to inspect a bungalow the firm was building on a small site near Watton. I had contacted *The Lynn News & Advertiser* about this, and it sent a very keen young representative called John Allen to collect the copy for what was to be my first advertisement. John rose through the ranks of Anglia Newspapers, eventually becoming managing director of the company, which was based in Bury St Edmunds. Many years later, I was privileged to attend his retirement party. Apart from our business dealings, we also shared the ups and downs of Ipswich Town Football Club. He died just a few months ago.

On Friday 7 October, the first advertisement for Bedford – The Estate Agents, appeared in *The Lynn News* and I formally opened the office. The advertisement featured three properties, including the cottage in Great Dunham.

The following week, I took two days off. On the Wednesday, we moved the furniture out of Hengrave into Foffum House. There was quite a bit of work to do in the kitchen and bathroom, so we only stored the furniture at that stage. Sadie and the two boys moved in with her parents in King's Lynn. I spent some nights there and others with my parents (when I needed a good night's sleep!). This unsatisfactory arrangement lasted nearly five weeks.

We finally moved into Foffum House over the weekend of 19 November. During those early weeks of my business, it is interesting how many of the friends I had made in Suffolk contacted me. Among them was Paul Rackham, of whom we'll hear more later. He gave me a couple of bungalows to sell in Sporle, a village just outside Swaffham.

Towards the end of October, I signed the lease for the office premises. That was about three weeks after we moved in! Then another developer, David Lloyd, who had built a huge estate of houses at Rougham, just outside Bury St Edmunds, called in one morning to ask about a site I had on my books. I told him where to find the land – it was in Sporle – and, in the afternoon, he came back and offered £9,000!

I was receiving a number of instructions in Mid-Norfolk – the area around Swaffham – but what surprised me was the number I was receiving in West Norfolk – from the area around King's Lynn. According to my diary, I had a meeting with John Gethin on 23 November about what we came to call "Operation K" – the opening of an office in King's Lynn. On 6 December, I had an appointment with the Midland Bank in the town, also regarding "Operation K."

This may all sound a bit rash but, by then, I was sure that Swaffham would succeed. This wasn't because of the properties I had already been asked to sell – it was because of those I could see down the line. A few weeks before I opened the office, I spotted Josh Bennett, of Bennetts the builders, on a ladder clipping his garden hedge while I was driving through Brandon to visit Swaffham, and stopped to have a word with him. Sometime before, I had learned that Bennetts was about to start work on an estate of 49 bungalows at Greenhoe Place in Swaffham. I had approached Josh's son-in-law, Lawrence Noble, about it. He had told me they would be selling them themselves, but would be happy to continue the same arrangement with me that they had had with Rutters – that is, that they would bear me in mind when it came to selling difficult plots.

Josh asked how I was getting on and, in particular, whether I had given my notice to Rutters. When I said I had, he asked when my new office would be up and running. He wished me well and, just as I was getting back into my car, added, "I think you had better sell the Greenhoe Place site for us. I'll get Lawrence to give you a call." Josh was a very shrewd old boy. He knew that, to have given me the bungalows to sell before I was committed to opening an office in Swaffham, would have made things far too easy for me. I have a lot to thank Josh Bennett for as, over the following two or three years, as well as the 49 Bennetts' bungalows in Swaffham, I sold 114 in Narborough (between Swaffham and

King's Lynn), 30 in Sporle, about 80 in Hockwold and 65 in East Harling!

In my first month at Swaffham, I sold four properties for commission totalling £343 15s 0d (£345.75). In the following month – November – I sold three and, in December, four. Despite this, my bank statement told me there was very little coming in and quite a lot going out. But success was just around the corner. In December 1966, I sold the first plot, number 86, at Westfields in Narborough for Bennetts for £2,520. It must have been a three bedroom bungalow as the fee was £50. I only got paid £40 for two-bedders!

Josh had set up Bennetts sometime in the late 1940s or early 1950s – I'm not sure exactly when. Starting in very modest premises in Lakenheath, the business expanded rapidly to meet the burgeoning demand for traditional detached bungalows, mainly from couples looking to retire to Norfolk from London and the Home Counties.

In October 1972, when he decided to retire, Josh sold the company to Nigel Parker, a developer from Essex. My older son, Paul, spent several years with the firm, gaining experience that would prove invaluable when we set up our specialist agency, Just Bungalows, but more of this later.

Nigel's company is now in the safe hands of his son, Edward, and operating from a head office near Bury St Edmunds.

Chapter 10

Lift Off!

While I was pleased to have sold 11 properties in the first three months of my business, 1967 turned out to be unbelievable. In January alone, I sold 23. In the calendar year from January to December, the total was 239. But at the start of the year, it was very much a hand-to-mouth existence. The process of agreeing a sale, instructing solicitors and exchanging contracts takes at least two months, after which there is at least another month before completion, when agents' fees get paid, so I was sweating about cash flow well into the spring. The £3,000 with which I started the business had virtually disappeared by then but, as January's bumper record of sales started to come through, the bank balance began to rise.

To open the office in King's Lynn, I rented one large room at 27 King Street, in a building I would share with the West Norfolk Conservative Association. It was next to The Guildhall which, even in those days, was the centre for The King's Lynn Festival – an event the Queen Mother regularly attended. I had employed another secretary for the King's Lynn office but, until later in that year, I was doing all the valuations, the preparations of sale particulars and most of the negotiations myself.

Back-office, I got my stepfather, Chris, to help. By then, he had retired from Shell and I roped him in as bookkeeper and accountant. I also bought him a second-hand pickup truck so he could go out and put up "For Sale" boards for me. I quite enjoyed putting them up myself, though, so I would often take Paul out to do it at the weekends. He was about four at the time, but the weekends clearly left a lasting impression. Later in the year, Sadie took him back to Bury St Edmunds to go to the pantomime at The Theatre Royal. When, as is often the case, the actors invited children up on stage, Paul was among them. When he was asked "What does your daddy do?" he promptly replied. "He carries boards around." Friends in the audience found it very amusing, especially when the host added "Oh, he has one of these sandwich boards, walking around advertising, does he?"

--- ooo ---

One of those instrumental in my success was Paul Rackham, who I mentioned earlier.

In 1967, I was approached by a local coal man who owned some fields on the southern edge of Swaffham. He thought they might have potential for housing and I offered to look into it for him. My memory may have faded, but I think the site plan I sent to the local planning office simply had a red line on it defining the boundary of the area in question. The planners came back with a few questions but, within six weeks, outline planning permission was granted for about 200 properties. Fifty years on, it would be a result if you achieved that in six years!

I telephoned Paul, who agreed to purchase the site subject to detailed planning, which took a further six months to obtain. Within a few days, Paul telephoned with devastating news: he had agreed to sell the site to another developer. However, he then confirmed he had made it a condition that I was appointed sole agent for the sale of all the properties on the development. The site was partly developed and then resold, but the condition withstood the scrutiny of various lawyers and I received a fee on every plot.

Property developers, particularly successful ones, get a bad press and I have been pleased to quote this story on many occasions, particularly when one of Paul's companies – a joint venture with a bank – got into trouble. It was the bank that went bust – hardly Paul's fault!

--- ooo ---

One of my colleagues at Rutters had been a young surveyor called John Rogers. He was running the firm's Thetford office, so I still came across him from time to time. There was a certain amount of overlap in the villages such as Mundford, where we occasionally had joint agencies.

One afternoon, John came to see me to say that the new Smiths Gore regime didn't suit him, and that he wondered if I had an opening. During the month of May 1967, I had sold 30 properties: 17 bungalows for Bennetts, either in Swaffham or at Westfields in Narborough, and nine other properties through my recently-opened office in King's Lynn. We had also received instructions from Barker Brothers, a well-established builder from Downham Market, to sell houses on a new estate in South Wootton. Sadie convinced me that I needed help, so I offered John the opportunity of running my King's Lynn office which, to my relief, he accepted.

Next to the old cattle market in King's Lynn, New Conduit Street and Broad Street contained many fine Georgian and Elizabethan properties and, every time I went to King's Lynn, I would see more "Acquired for Clients by Harry Ball" signs in those streets. Today, most of those buildings would be listed, but King's Lynn was to be the first of many towns to fall for the promise that redevelopment was the key to its future. You will remember that, in an earlier chapter, I said the storm clouds were not yet gathering. Well, by now, they had – and with a vengeance! Whole streets of beautiful listed buildings were bulldozed, only to be replaced by the most hideous new developments. With the benefit of nearly 50 years' hindsight, King's Lynn has never really recovered. The council and planning authorities must take the blame.

Saturday Market Place, King Street, Queen Street and Tuesday Market Place, still give a flavour of what the town used to be. The rest is now a very poor imitation of Croydon – and I say that with apologies to the residents of that town! The wonderful gents' outfitters, Jones & Dunn, and the fine grocer's and coffee shop, Ladymans, are gone, and many other cherished buildings are just a distant memory.

It's a mark of its success – or, rather, its lack of it – that the 1960s development has since been redeveloped itself, mainly because shops there were unlettable. Unfortunately, the updated scheme is barely an improvement on the original. Today, King's Lynn must have one of the highest numbers of unoccupied shops in the Eastern Counties. I can't help comparing it with Bury St Edmunds, where I live today. Some ten years ago, the council there proposed a new development on Cattle Market. Recalling what happened to King's Lynn, I was not just anxious, I was a very vocal opponent. The scheme was completed around the time that banks started crashing in 2008. Tempted by incentives including rent-free periods, some of the national chains moved into The Arc, as the shopping centre was called. That left a lot of empty shops in Buttermarket and Cornhill, the traditional shopping area of the town. But as the economy has improved, I have been happy to eat humble pie. I can't think of any other town that could absorb a new Debenhams and 35 other new shops in the teeth of one of the deepest recessions of our time and still finish up with very few empty shops.

The development includes a beautiful concert hall, The Apex, but the council sadly ignored professional advice that it should have at least a thousand seats and built it with half that number. Bury's lovely Georgian Theatre Royal was already struggling to fill its 350 seats, and The Apex just made matters worse. It competes to stage the same scale of production. A larger-capacity venue would have attracted much larger productions into the town, and a different audience to go with them.

--- 000 ---

To return to the opening of my King's Lynn office, once John was installed, I only needed to go over once or twice a week to meet specific clients. Because of the redevelopment work, it was like a

building site. The traffic was impossible so, until, I think, the end
of 1968, I used to regularly catch the train there from Swaffham.
It wasn't quite The Orient Express, but it was a very pleasant
journey, stopping in Narborough and East Winch before arriving
at King's Lynn. Sadly, it was one of the early lines to be struck by
Mr Beeching's axe.

Foffum House was the fifth house we had lived in during our
married life. For the first year or 18 months, it served its purpose.
It was just round the corner from the office so, at busy times, the
telephone could be diverted to the house and Sadie could help
answer calls. She also became the office cleaner – the best-paid
cleaner in Norfolk!

The move from a very comfortable and attractive house in
Hengrave to a pretty ordinary property on a main road in
Swaffham wasn't something every wife would have put up with
but, to her credit, Sadie never complained. I was so busy building
the business that it didn't occur to me that we should move to
somewhere better.

One evening, though, a local GP, Mike Pilkington, whom
Sadie and I had met on one or two occasions, came into the office
to say he had a scheme he thought I might be interested in. He had
quite a pleasant house in London Street, but the traffic there was
getting busier. With a growing family, he also needed somewhere
a bit bigger. The property he had found was on the Norwich Road.
It included a derelict farmhouse – Rookery Farm – three acres of
land and some very scruffy buildings, and had been on the market
for some time.

Mike took me to see the property the following day. We parked the car and ventured cautiously onto a site which, to say the least, was overgrown. The nettles and brambles were head height. Fortunately, he had come prepared with gardening gloves for both of us, a hook and an improvised machete. Suitably equipped, we fought our way up a gentle south-facing slope to the top of the site. On our way up, we found a rusty lorry chassis without the cab and an old van!

But the location was magnificent. Mike wanted to build a new house at the top of the site, but it was the farmhouse that appealed to me. I wanted to restore it. The site was more or less rectangular, and we produced a crude plan, splitting it into four quarters. Front left was the farmhouse, front right were some other farm buildings and top right was the plot Mike wanted. Top left was an area we thought we would jointly own and put down as a paddock.

I was happy with the work John Whisson had done on the office, but I had no particularly preference for architects locally. Mike and his partners had recently completed work on a new surgery building in Swaffham and he was anxious to introduce me to Sheila and Michael Gooch, a couple from Norwich with an excellent reputation as architects. While Mike was contacting the Gooches, I spoke with Noel Abel, the agent for the site, which had been one of his "best-kept secrets." Mike and I had decided to make an offer. We were pretty confident we'd get permission to build at least one new property on the site and do up the farmhouse, so we didn't make it subject to planning permission. I agreed a deal with Noel and instructed a firm of solicitors.

Contracts were quickly exchanged, but we managed to delay completion for six months, by which time we hoped we would have been given planning permission and have secured a loan to pay for the property.

To start with, the planners told Sheila they thought the farmhouse was beyond repair and should be demolished. They were, however, sympathetic to the construction of a new house, so plans for what would become Mike's and his wife's home were drawn up and submitted. On the site plan, the curtilage that was to be Mike's garden was shown as being his property, while the remainder of the farm would be owned by others. This was nearly correct. On completion, I was going to take ownership of the farmhouse and the rest of the site was going to be in our joint names. The planners were still telling Sheila they expected the farmhouse to be demolished but (fortuitously!), when consent for Mike's new house was granted, there was no condition to this effect. Communication within the council's offices clearly wasn't all that good at the time! Hoping the loophole wouldn't be closed, I immediately instructed Sheila to prepare plans for the renovation and extension of the farmhouse, which was quite a prominent building on the approach to Swaffham. We were delighted when consent was granted.

--- ooo ---

The business was doing extremely well, so I was able to fund the conversion of Rookery Farm by taking some cash out of the firm and asking the bank for a bit of help. Mike and Mary had already completed their house and moved in. We managed to sell Foffum House and the adjoining property to a local landowner, who converted the two into a shop with flats over the top. For many years now, the ground floor has been the Woods family's gun and sports shop.

With the business increasing month on month and the extra pressure of overseeing the renovation of Rookery Farm, life got very hectic. In urgent need of a break, Sadie and I left Paul and James in the care of their grannies and flew abroad for a two-week holiday. When I came back, I was surprised to find that John Rogers, who you'll remember was running my King's Lynn office, had changed his car. We parted company shortly after this. Cars are the source of far too many problems in business!

One of the best advertising campaigns of the 1970s – a "game changer".

Chapter 11

Rush Hour, Norfolk Style

In early 1968, I opened a third office. This one was in Downham Market.

Although I had taken on more staff, the sacking of John Rogers had left me under a great deal of stress. The previous year, I had met a keen young pipe-smoking assistant who worked for Long & Beck, a long-established auctioneer in Fakenham. His name was Chris Pointen and, like me, he was a hockey player. One day, I bumped into him in the bar at Dereham Hockey Club. He made it quite clear that he saw no future with Long & Beck. Most of its income came from a lively market every Thursday that included a furniture sale room.

Hoping he would help solve my problem, I offered Chris a job. He very quickly joined me at Swaffham, moving to the town with his wife, Yvonne, shortly afterwards. I had employed another manager at King's Lynn, who was okay, but not memorable enough for me to remember his name. Once Chris was up to speed in Swaffham, I was able to devote more time to business elsewhere, in King's Lynn and Downham Market.

My original secretary at King's Lynn was a lovely lady called Christine Fletcher who, at that time, lived with her parents in a railway cottage in Denver, near Downham Market, where her father had been a level-crossing operator since long before the line was electrified. When I opened the Downham Market office,

Christine was keen to move there, but I persuaded her to stay in King's Lynn and employed another excellent secretary, Sandra Haynes, to work there instead.

Like Swaffham, Downham Market had several new estates, predominantly of bungalows. Together with the other Bennetts sites around the county, this accounted for a large part of my firm's business. Many of the purchasers came from the northern suburbs of London, Essex and Hertfordshire. The railway line to London allowed them to move to Norfolk without losing touch with friends and relatives.

Bedfords was one of the first firms to tap this market using national advertising. The main publications we used were *Daltons Weekly* and *Home Finder Magazine*. By the late 1960s and early 1970s, the firm was also attending the latter's annual New Homes Exhibition. Exhibitions like that were hard work and expensive. The train service wasn't brilliant back then, so we had to put staff up in London hotels.

Our advertising campaigns were a big success. One of the most successful came to me while I was driving through Brandon one day on my way from Bury to Swaffham. These days, it would fall foul of various pieces of consumer legislation, but we ran it for several years.

With the idea in my mind, I turned off the main road onto the dead-straight secondary road that leads to Grimes Grave, parked the car, walked 50 yards down the road and took a photograph that showed nothing but the forest and my car. The advertisement featured the photograph and a strap line – "rush hour, Norfolk-style." These days, there are some very clever and sophisticated advertisements, but "rush hour" did the job for me. Not only did it help the firm sell properties, it attracted several new developer clients, one of which was Kerridges of Cambridge, for which we sold homes in Narborough and Hunstanton.

It never ceased to amaze me how many retired couples would decide to move to Norfolk, leaving their friends and families. Financially, it made a lot of sense, of course. They would probably have sold a semi-detached house in, say, Romford for £25,000 and only had to pay £5,000 for a nice detached bungalow much closer to countryside. Some did have relatives in the area, but most had only very tenuous connections to Norfolk. The husband might have spent time at Marham or West Raynham while he was in the RAF, or the family might have enjoyed an odd week's holiday in Sheringham or Hunstanton. Having seen one of our advertisements, they would telephone to arrange a date and time to visit. Some would come by car, but others would come by train and have to be met at Brandon, Downham Market or King's Lynn. After visiting the site they were interested in and selecting a plot, they would come to one of our offices to pay the £50 deposit. The arrangement we had with Bennetts, which formed the bulk of our sales for the first few years, was that plots would be sold "bare" to start with, but subject to contracts for bungalows to be built afterwards. Purchasers would pay in stages as construction of the property progressed. It was a very neat arrangement. The costs of construction were financed by the purchaser, so the builder had to borrow much less cash up-front. Purchasers benefitted as well. While some had savings, most would have to sell an existing home to complete the purchase of their new property. Thanks to the staging arrangement, they didn't have to do this immediately. Another neat twist was that, when purchasers sold their existing homes before their new ones were ready for occupation, Bennetts could rent one of the properties it owned in the area to them to tide them over. It worked like a dream!

Over the months and years, prices inevitably crept up. I clearly remember Laurence Noble, then sales director at Bennetts, ringing me up to say a board meeting had decided to increase the minimum price for a two bedroom bungalow to just over £4,000. We had managed to keep the "from" price at £3,950 for some time. Convinced it would be the end for both our businesses if prices went over the £4,000 mark, I jumped in my car and drove to Bennetts' office in Lakenheath where I plead with Laurence and another director, Les Rutterford, not to go ahead. History has proved me wrong: bungalows like that sell for around £250,000 these days!

--- ooo ---

Sadie, the boys and I had settled into Rookery Farm but, while the house was extremely comfortable, the garden was simply a ploughed field. Sadie knew what she wanted and set about providing interest and colour. My contribution was to ensure that there weren't too many corners to the lawn so I could treat myself to a ride-on mower and be responsible for the stripes.

Paul was attending the local convent school and James, I seem to recall, was attending two or three mornings a week.

Our social life mainly revolved around Pelicans Hockey Club. However, most Friday evenings there would be a "boys" get-together in The George Hotel in Swaffham and it was there that I first met John Bucher and Martin Lang, both of whom are still good friends.

When she left school, my sister Mary worked for a time in Jermyns, King's Lynn, and then for a firm of solicitors in the town – Kenneth Bush & Co. As I'm sure all brothers and sisters do, we fought quite a lot when we were young. In the days when I would head back to King's Lynn from Bury at the weekends, Sadie would often spend the Saturday night at my parents' house, sharing a bedroom with Mary who, at that time, was still at school. After everyone had gone to bed, Sadie would creep along the corridor to say "good night" to me with "Don't be long, otherwise I shall tell my mummy" ringing in her ears!

My sister became friendly with several of the members at the hockey club, including a rather noisy farmer from The Fens called Martin Goodley. In time, they became what, in current parlance, is referred to as "an item" and, although on the one hand I was pleased for her, I began to think his intentions were not honourable. I can't remember the exact circumstances but, one night in the pub, I got upset and poured a pint of beer over his head. He didn't seem to mind, but Mary was furious. No lasting damage was done and, early in 1969, they got engaged.

Mother and Chris lived in a modest bungalow in Swaffham with a smallish garden, so Sadie and I were happy to suggest that the reception should be at Rookery Farm. There was space for a marquee on our wonderful lawn which, thanks to my new mower, boasted immaculate stripes. Everybody was happy with this arrangement, so Mary and Martin were duly married at St Peter and St Paul's Church, Swaffham, on 26 September 1969. James and Paul were page boys and I was an usher, along with Alan Cargill, Bill Everington and David Johnson. Sadly, Bill and David are no longer with us.

Some of you reading this book may start wondering what happened to my sister. Shortly after they were married, Martin christened her "Bumble," due to her habit of rushing around and, as he put it, bumbling like a bee. The name stuck, so I'll be using it from here.

--- ooo ---

Despite our involvement with Pelicans and with Norfolk in general, we regularly revisited Bury St Edmunds for functions and balls in The Athenaeum that had names like "The Gay Bachelors," "The March Hares" and, one that I was involved in, "The Reapers." You didn't have to be gay, mad or grim to join in!

Eight or ten of us would be involved in the organisation, hiring the room, caterers and band, and each of us would invite his or her own guests. The Reapers was basically aimed at farmers and hangers-on, like agents!

I remember Peter Morton, a farmer from Norton, driving his tractor and trailer into town laden with straw bales – the old rectangular ones – which we spread around The Athenaeum to give the required rustic atmosphere and create seating around the dance floor. The majority of us smoked, so it was a miracle that The Athenaeum wasn't burnt down. You'd have to fire-proof the bales these days!

Back in Swaffham, John Burton, the clerk to the rural district council, invited me and a few others to a meeting. It had been suggested that Swaffham should form a Rotary Club. Along with John, I remember Ken Reeve, a local bank manager, Graham Chapman, who was with the local agriculture firm, Plowrights, and Mike Pilkington, my neighbour, coming along. Over the course of several meetings, the names of various prospective members were put forward. Some accepted when they were asked, but others were not so keen. Bearing in mind you could be a member of The Round Table until the age of 40 and that most of my contemporaries were still in their thirties, their reaction was "I'm not old enough!"

The Rotary also had fairly strict rules as to who could, and who could not, be a member. For example, clubs could only have one member from each trade or profession. In some cases that was easier than in others. You could break my trade down into estate agents, valuers, surveyors and auctioneers so our club could – and indeed did – have one of each.

Having retired from being the Chaplain to the Queen at Sandringham, Canon Hugh Blackburn had just moved into The Old Rectory in Cockley Cley and was helping out with several parishes to the south of Swaffham. Having found out that he had been an active Rotarian, we invited him to become a member and help with the setting up of the club, which he did. A while later, somebody proposed the local vicar, Neil Mash, as a member. I remember John Burton holding up his hand and saying, "Hang on, we've already got Hugh as a member." He was also in the religious trade, after all. But Hugh immediately responded: "No problem! Neil is retail and I'm wholesale!"

With Hugh's experience in Rotary, we soon recruited the required number of members and the club was formed. In 1974, I became its fourth president. At that time, our lunches were held on a Monday at The George Hotel. I have some good memories of my time in Rotary but, along with one or two others, didn't take it quite as seriously as perhaps I should have done.

Among the members was Dennis Woodhams, the manager of The George, who had a wicked sense of humour. Norman Phillips, who ran a successful garage in town, was a charming guy of the old school. Because he always wore a beret, he reminded many of us of a French farmer. On one occasion when Norman was absent, when it came to "Any Other Business," Dennis stood up and, with a very straight face, announced that he thought all members would like to join with him in wishing Norman a speedy recovery. This came as a bit of a shock – we had no idea he was ill – and, eventually, one of us asked what the nature of Norman's illness was. It would be hard to forget Dennis' reply: "Oh, he's not ill. He's just having an operation for the removal of his beret!"

--- ooo ---

Throughout all this, Bedfords continued to grow. Chris Pointen was helping at Swaffham but, sooner or later, I was going to need someone at the Downham Market office as well. Having no one in mind, I placed an advertisement in *Estates Gazette*.

Among the applicants was a young man called Chris Nash. Originally from Norfolk, he had been training with an auctioneer in Yorkshire. First impressions were good, so I invited him to an interview. That's when I discovered he was a very good hockey player. As I've joked with him many times since, Pelicans needed a centre half, so I had to give him the job!

Producing our own publications for nearly forty years.

Chapter 12

The 1970s

The 1970s proved to be a rollercoaster decade. The property market had its ups and downs: Bedfords' business grew dramatically; Sadie and I acquired a beautiful family house – one my brother-in-law described as a "proper house" at the time; the firm bought a fine new head office; and then, just before the end of the decade, the partnership, Bedford – The Estate Agent, was dissolved, leaving me happier, but with just two offices.

By the end of the 1960s, the offices in Swaffham, King's Lynn and Downham Market were doing extremely well. In 1969, they sold nearly 400 properties; in 1970, it was 540.

Chris Nash and Chris Pointen were enthusiastically helping me develop the business, but there wasn't anything you could really call a business plan. We were flying by the seat of our pants! Financial decisions were made on the back of an envelope. Stepfather Chris was struggling to keep up with the accounts: he wasn't in the best of health and really wanted to retire again! We had run out of space in the Swaffham office and had no room for additional staff, and the organisation and erection of "For Sale" and "Sold" boards was proving a real headache. In those days, we couldn't just farm the work out to agencies that would do it for us.

I think it was Mike Pilkington who told me that one of his former partners, who had retired, was moving to a smaller house from his present one, The Hollies. Located in London Street,

Swaffham, it was a fine Georgian property that included spacious living accommodation and a former surgery, lovely walled garden, cottage and a barn. I believe it was on the market for £15,000 but, after some negotiation with the agents, Savills, I bought it for about £13,000. I thought it would make a magnificent office with plenty of room not just for the back-up staff we already needed, but for the extra hands that would be needed to expand the business.

Once again, I instructed Michael and Sheila Gooch as architects. They prepared an imaginative plan to add a reception area with display windows that would front onto what was to become the car park. Despite several colleagues and friends warning of the dangers of "decentralising," leaving the market square in Swaffham was a successful move. The Hollies was prominent on the approach to Swaffham and, even in those days, parking in the town centre was a bit of a problem. The new building had its own car park.

After acquiring the office late in 1969, Sadie and I, together with our good friends, Tim and Mieneke Gregorie, Mervyn and Joanna Gribbon and Robert and Margo Pickering, decided to take advantage of the spacious empty rooms to hold a party. Having decided on a theme – "Sail into the 1970s" – we invited friends to enjoy a "naughty nautical night." It was a memorable occasion! Everyone entered into the spirit of the evening, dressing up accordingly or, in the case of a lovely local lady JP, doing virtually the opposite!

Plans for the office alterations were passed but, although I thought I had bought a bit of a bargain, the costs of conversion started to rise. To the rear of the property, a large kitchen garden fronted onto another street. To make sure I had enough to cover all the costs, I sought permission to build five town houses there. Once the council had given its approval, I sold the land to Walter Lawrence, a large local firm of building contractors. The managing director was Ken Wall, who became a great friend. His son – who is still in the property business – is a client of Bedfords' Burnham Market office.

Alterations and refurbishment complete, the Swaffham office moved into The Hollies in January 1972.

The firm was not the only thing that was expanding. Just after the decade started, Sadie fell pregnant again. Michael, our third son, was born in October 1970. While Rookery Farm had been a wonderful and comfortable home, the imminent expansion of our family meant we had to consider building on another bedroom and playroom. The plans were duly passed and I began talking to a local builder regarding an estimate.

One of the best-kept secrets in Swaffham was Holmwood House. Situated behind a high wall, it had 40 acres of beautiful grounds, parkland and farmland. The owner, a retired tea planter – Claude Bois, opened the grounds for the church fete and other charitable events. Sadie and I had met him on one or two occasions. As far as I can remember, he had been a widower with a grown-up family, but he had recently remarried by then. His new wife was a charming lady called Elizabeth, who had a house near East Dereham.

One gloomy November afternoon, Claude invited me to call in for a cup of tea. He introduced me to Elizabeth, who had a property to sell, and said they would like me to deal with it. During the conversation – it took place over Dundee Cake – it emerged that he was also planning to sell his Holmwood House. They would be moving to a new house under construction near Elgin in Morayshire, Scotland. Claude explained that, while he would have very much liked me to sell the house for him, he had instructed Charles Hawkins & Sons of King's Lynn, the firm that always acted for him. The penny dropped that I was being offered the consolation prize – selling Elizabeth's house – but then an opportunity dawned on me. Bearing in mind our situation, I said that Sadie and I might be interested in the house for ourselves. He suggested I should telephone Sadie immediately, but I thought it would be better to talk to her about it face-to-face and come back the following day. That we did. Both Sadie and I thought Holmwood House would make a great home for our family. The wonderful garden, which she had seen the previous summer, also appealed. It was a very foggy afternoon so we never really saw the land, but we knew roughly how far it extended. Claude said he "thought" the price was about £40,000 and I confirmed our interest. He picked up the telephone, spoke to Gordon Brown, a partner at Hawkins I knew well, and told him "Friends of mine want to buy the house. They will be in touch with you tomorrow." After he put the phone down, he told me that the tenant who farmed most of the land had offered a low figure on the property a few weeks before, but he thought they had just been "messing around." He would much rather we bought it. Claude had always had a twinkle in his eye as far as Sadie was concerned, so that may have helped!

I rang Gordon the following day. He was most polite, but clearly somewhat uncomfortable in view of the negotiations that had been going on with the farmer. I asked what the price was and he said they were looking for something "around £40,000." I gathered from Claude Bois that, while they wanted to exchange contracts, they didn't want to move until the following autumn, when their Scottish property would be finished. On that basis, I offered to pay £42,000, exchange contracts without delay and to agree the completion date later in the year. The last point was very important, as I had already bought The Hollies with no idea where the money was coming from. A couple of hours later, Claude Bois telephoned me to say, despite the "shit hitting the fan" and counter offers having been made, he wanted us to have the house. We metaphorically shook hands on the deal over the phone.

The 1970s were off to a great start. Just a few months in and we had bought two of the finest properties in the town – one for business, one for pleasure.

--- ooo ---

Since starting my own business, I had maintained a good relationship with Midland Bank. I was on first-name terms with the various managers. Looking back, this was fortunate. When it came to buying properties, I had what, these days, I would describe as a rather cavalier approach! I would exchange contracts and talk to the bank afterwards – the exact opposite of what most people would think made sense.

When I bought Holmwood House, my luck held out again. I explained how, after committing to buy The Hollies, I was able to sell off the kitchen garden and a small cottage to give me the money I needed to complete the project. When committing to Holmwood House, I had about six or seven months between exchanging contracts and completion – the point at which I would have to hand over the cash. I was fairly confident that Rookery Farm would sell, but my personal ambition overrode a good agent's advice. I set the price too high, so the property hung around on the market for several months.

In the meantime, the local council was looking for a play-area-cum-football-pitch for a school just up the road from Holmwood House. In between were about a dozen local authority houses with very deep gardens. I suggested to the council that, if they halved the depths of these gardens, which would still leave the houses with spaces that were more than adequate, I had a suitable area of land next to them that I was prepared to sell. It was screened from Holmwood House by a wood, so the impact on our home would be minimal. Luckily, the council liked the idea. The district valuer agreed to pay me £20,000 for the land, which was half what I was paying for the entire property. The house needed a tremendous amount of money spending on it but, with the eventual sale of Rookery Farm and this windfall, we managed to pay for everything.

Foolishly, there was one item I didn't replace at the time – the boiler. Installed in the cellar, the huge device had originally been designed to burn coke, but had been converted to run on oil. As the 1973 oil crisis approached, the running costs had become astronomical. The conclusion was clear – the boiler would have to be replaced, and the sooner the better! In the end, the decision was taken out of my hands. A couple of months after we moved into the house, the heating suddenly went off. The lining of the chimney that acted as the flue to the boiler had collapsed.

At the time, we were constructing a swimming pool in the garden. The boiler we needed to heat the water was to be housed in an outbuilding and powered by gas. Sadie was never keen on having gas in our houses – before we moved into Holmwood House, she had insisted that the gas cooker was replaced with an electric one – but I persuaded her that we should have a gas boiler for the heating as well. The inefficiency of British Gas at the time meant that the last step of the work to remove the cooker and cut off the supply – the cancellation of our account – happened after the new boilers had been installed and the supply reconnected. We enjoyed a very comfortable warm house and a swimming pool heated to a very pleasant temperature, oblivious to the fact that we never got a bill.

When the new office in Swaffham was opened, I employed an accountant to replace my stepfather, Chris. I used to take most of the household bills to the office so that they could be paid with company cheques debited against my drawings. We had been in Holmwood House about a year when the accountant, Graham Hardy, said he couldn't find any record of us having had a gas bill. I didn't feel like ringing up British Gas to ask for one, so the situation continued and I became increasingly worried about the size of the gas bill that might eventually turn up. We lived at

Holmwood for about ten years, but British Gas never did send a bill!

They were obviously aware that something was wrong, though. On one occasion, contractors came to look for what British Gas must have decided was a leak from the main. Over the course of a couple of weeks, they dug a trench down the whole length of the road to lay a new main. I went home for lunch one day and wandered out to chat with the workmen. Wanting to be helpful, I pointed out where the pipe leading into my property went. I thought Holmwood House was probably the "leak," but they didn't seem to care!

--- ooo ---

Despite all the action on the property front – the new office and the move to Holmwood – Bedfords managed to open an office in Hunstanton, then, in 1972, another in Fakenham. Stephen Crossley joined us to run the Hunstanton office and Chris Nash, who had done extremely well in Downham Market, took over Fakenham. He was keen to move nearer Mid Norfolk and had volunteered to move there.

To run the Downham Market office, we recruited a chap called John Deans. Although he worked hard and produced results, I remember that the very first time Sadie met him, she told me "I don't trust him."

Brian Paton, a chartered surveyor, had joined us at King's Lynn. He was very professional and developed a good practice carrying out surveys and similar, but I felt we needed someone with a bit more drive to develop sales in West Norfolk, particularly at Lynn and the new office at Hunstanton.

Over five years, the business had grown from just me and a secretary to employ more than 20 staff. Across our five offices, we were selling something like a thousand houses a year. It was a big achievement, and I was immensely grateful to Sadie for supporting me throughout, but a lot of capital was now tied up in the business and I was carrying the responsibility for the whole enterprise. It was quite a lonely place to be!

It was at this time that seeds were sown of problems that would materialise later on.

The business was doing extremely well and generating good profits, so I decided that I should invite Chris Pointen to become a partner, which he appreciated, and this was shortly followed by my inviting Brian Paton to become a partner, mainly because I felt I needed to "lock" senior people in. Then, late in 1972 or early in 1973, I saw an advertisement in *The Estates Gazette*. Placed by a young surveyor from Sheffield, it said he was looking for a position with a progressive firm in East Anglia. I replied and received an interesting letter, together with a CV, from a young man called Harry Hill. I invited him to come to Swaffham for an interview and had a good feeling about him straightaway. While very direct, I thought the Yorkshireman would be a valuable addition to the business. Because he was married with a young family, which would make it a big move for him, I suggested he and his wife should come down for a weekend to make sure they were comfortable with the area. I hadn't mentioned my meeting with Harry to Chris or Brian as I was worried, particularly in

Brian's case, what their reactions would be. They would want to know where the new man would fit in. But I really wanted another opinion before finally offering Harry the job, so Sadie and I invited him and his wife to dinner on the Saturday night, together with our good friends Tim and Mieneke Gregorie. Mieneke was a very forthright Dutch lady and the evening was a great success. The "Yorkshire versus Holland" match was a score draw, and Harry clearly passed both the Sadie and Mieneke tests! Some years later, he told me that, during the dinner party, he had calculated that our dining room furniture and a few pictures were worth more than his house in Yorkshire! Harry was to go on to become CEO of Countrywide, so he was no fool. He was just a better estate agent than furniture valuer!

Having accepted my offer of employment, Harry moved his family to Dersingham, midway between King's Lynn and Hunstanton. His enthusiasm was soon reflected in the performance of the offices in the two towns. To help, he recruited David Fletcher, a young man from Barclays Bank who adapted quickly to Bedfords and was to prove an important member of staff, not just for us but for Harry in his years at Countrywide.

Left:
Gage Cottage,
Hengrave.
Our first home.

Below: The
receipt for the
£80 deposit!

No.   BURY ST. EDMUNDS   February 12th 1960

ARTHUR RUTTER, SONS & CO.,
Chartered Auctioneers and Estate Agents

Received of Mr D. J. Bedford   the
Sum of Eighty _____ Pounds
                Shillings _____ Pence, being
Interest deposit + first payment purchase of 5 Bury Road
Hengrave   freehold

£ 80 : :   Subject to formal
              Contract

Above: Gage House, Hengrave.
Centre inset: Sadie, Paul and myself in the garden at Gage house.

Above: 1966. My first Instruction. Point House, Great Dunham. Off to a flying start!!!

Above: "Foffum House" as named by Paul.

Above: Rookery Farm, Swaffham.

Above: Holmwood House, Swaffham. while living here, in 1979 I turned off the "money tap"!

Above: 1992. Back "home" in Suffolk – Malting Farm, Dalham.

Above: Garland Lodge. We were one of the first "bungalow eaters" in the 1990s.

Inset left: Original property.

Below: Burnham Market office. "Lyons Tea", top left of window, a reminder of the former "Fortnum & Mason" in North Norfolk.

Above: Back to Bury St Edmunds. Number 81 Guildhall Street, this recent drawing by Martin Lightfoot shows the impressive offices of Bankes Ashton (now Ashton's Legal). My office in 1982 occupied the room on the right.

Below: 15 Guildhall Street, refurbished from original (inset left) in 1983, still occupied by the Bury St Edmunds office.

Above: How rumours start! Michael at Highclere Castle in 1992.

Paul (left) and me (below), providing market comment for local BBC TV.

'Tonight on Downton Abbey, 50 new houses are built on the front lawn'

Chapter 13

Inflation, House Prices
& Absent Friends

Launched in1970, Concorde was a symbol of that time. The rate it took off certainly reflected in the meteoric rises in inflation and house prices! In 1970, inflation was 5.9 percent and the average house price £4,975. Just four years later, inflation had risen to 17.2 percent and the average house price had doubled to £10,990. The era also saw the end of The Beatles (1970), the introduction of decimalisation (1971), the Watergate scandal (1972) and the Yom Kippur War (1973). The 200 percent increase in oil prices that resulted from the latter triggered a recession, a three-day week and the miners' strike. It is hard to describe how difficult times were then, with no power in the office for half the week, but fortunately we were still using "steam" typewriters and writing notes and instructions by hand. Work carried on by candlelight.

Despite this, the first years of the 1970s were good for Bedfords. The five offices were all generating good business and, even after drawing enough to enjoy a very comfortable lifestyle, the firm always maintained a healthy bank balance. It owned the freehold of The Hollies, and all the other offices were on good leases at sensible rents, so the firm was in a very strong position to survive the recession when it hit. I have my solicitor, John

Gethin, and my accountant, John Wildbur, to thank for much of that.

Although the sale of retirement bungalows was probably, in today's jargon, our "core" business, we also dealt with a lot of interesting properties and, indeed, some very interesting clients. Lady Evershed, the widow of a former Master of the Rolls, was one of them. She lived in Castle Acre, a village just north of Swaffham. At that time, the village had a reputation for being a bit rough. If there was a fight on a Saturday night in a pub in Fakenham, it would be reported in the press as having been "ten miles from Castle Acre"!

Keen to improve the village, Lady Evershed occasionally purchased a rundown cottage to refurbish. One sunny spring day, she invited me to advise her on a small cottage. Afterwards, while we were strolling around the green, she asked me how much I thought it was worth. I seem to recall telling her that, given Castle Acre's reputation, the answer was probably about £8,000. "I know exactly what you mean, Mr Bedford," she replied. "When I was young, I remember an elderly relative saying that, whenever he visited a brothel in London, there would always be a girl from Castle Acre there!!" The village is much sought after these days. Over the years, I have enjoyed telling this story to friends who have lived there!

--- ooo ---

In the early days of the business, I had always run a sensible car, usually a Ford. Now in my early thirties, I fancied something a little sportier, so I bought an MGB GT. With a wife and two children, it was wholly impractical – Paul and James only just managed to squeeze in the back – and I had only had it a few months when Sadie said she was pregnant again. Despite the car's limitations, Sadie (by then just two months away from giving birth to our son, Michael), Paul, James and I squeezed in and enjoyed a wonderful holiday in the summer of 1970, touring Ireland. We had to strap the suitcase to the roof!

That was the end of the road as far as the car was concerned. I had bought it from a salesman at Mann Egerton in King's Lynn who I had thought was rather pompous at the time, but I went to see him and told him about my problem. I remember to this day the classic line he uttered: "We find MGs do this sir!"

Amongst our good friends in Suffolk were Peter and Mary Cawston. Peter had worked for a firm in Newmarket from which I had once bought a second-hand Mini. He had recently moved to Cecil & Larter, one of Bury's long-established car dealers. When I called him, he was very excited – it was 1970, and the firm had just acquired the franchise for Volvo cars. I was the very first customer to buy one and took delivery after enjoying a summer Sunday lunch with friends, Ben and Jo Robbins. Peter opened the garage up especially to hand the new car over to me. Sadly, he died at an early age, but he would be pleased and proud to know not only that the firm is still prospering under the guidance of his son, Ray, but that his daughter, Anna, now runs a successful chain of fashion boutiques.

While the Volvo – it was a vivid yellow – did the job as far as the family was concerned, I was never really happy with it. In the summer of 1971, Sadie and I, together with Sandy Hills and his girlfriend at the time, Pat, drove it all the way to the South of France for a holiday in a caravan near St Tropez that belonged to a farmer client of Sandy's.

There are two things I particularly remember from that holiday. While we were sunbathing on the beach, a well-endowed girl was lying topless just a few yards away, much to the annoyance of Sadie and Pat. Deciding we needed a closer look, Sandy and I followed her into the sea when she went for a swim. A bit of underwater swimming allowed us to view her from a different angle! The following evening, we were strolling along the quay of the harbour in St Tropez, where all the wonderful yachts were moored and there was this young "lady," clearly on the "game." With much satisfaction, the girls told us "We knew she was a tart." The other memory is of the toilet block at the caravan site. Like most French establishments, the pan did not have a seat, so I bought a blow-up ring to take there on my visits. Sandy managed to take a photograph of me one day, coming out with it under my arm.

--- ooo ---

The following year, Sadie and I went on a wonderful sailing holiday with Mieneke and Tim Gregorie. After flying from Heathrow to Nice, we were transported to the marina. Having enjoyed a week's sailing, we then flew home, all for just £69 a head. The highlight of the trip was that Tim, who was an experienced sailor, had insisted on taking his weatherproof "oillies." One day we encountered the Mistral – the sometimes-violent wind that blows from France into the Mediterranean. Tim donned his weatherproof kit while the rest of us cowered in the cabin below.

Each evening, we would tie up in a marina and find a local restaurant for a meal. While in one such establishment, I needed an urgent visit to the lavatory. Having done what I needed to do, I discovered there was no toilet paper. When I got back to the table, I explained this. Mieneke asked what I had done, so I calmly informed her I had used a 10Fr note instead. She never let me forget it!

Many years later Mieneke and Tim were living in mid Norfolk when I was asked to sell a substantial house opposite their home.The new occupant ,Annie Tempest , became know to readers of Country Life Magazine as the creator of the ,much loved ,Tottering-By- Gently cartoons .

Many of us suspected the main character "Daffy" had a passing resemblance to Mieneke, recently confirmed by Annie in a TV documentary. "Min" as her friends referred to her sadly died a few years ago, but I enjoy a weekly reminder of her when my copy of the magazine drops through the letter box.

--- ooo ---

In the summer of 1971, Sandy Hills, who at that time lived in the mill in Kersey in Suffolk, invited us down for a week's holiday. Having a young family at the time, it was exactly what we needed, allowing us to meet up not just with Sandy, but with some of our Bury friends.

Before visiting Kersey, I had seen an advertisement in local lifestyle magazine, *East Anglian Life*, for a BMW 2002. The advertisement was a sketch showing the car in the rear view mirror of a car in front. The caption read "Move over."

The only dealer at the time was Cars Continental in Ipswich so, leaving Sadie and the children behind, I went into Ipswich one afternoon. I eventually found a garage that was, quite literally, a garage. It only had room for a car and a desk! But what a car it was! I was very impressed with the vehicle and went for a test drive. The salesman said the price was "about £1,500," so I asked him to write with a firm figure. When the letter arrived a couple of days later, I was horrified to find that the price was almost exactly what the name of the car might suggest – £2,002. Everything was an extra! My knee-jerk reaction was to write back and say "Forget it," which is what I did but, really, I wanted one. One evening while I was idly looking out of the window of Rookery Farm, a bus trundled past with an advert for Sycamores, the BMW garage in Peterborough, on its side. That did it! The next day, I drove to Peterborough and bought my first BMW. My friends thought I was mad! The small two-door vehicle had cost as much as a Jaguar XJ saloon.

A few weeks later, our great friend, Martin Laing was about to get married. I offered to drive him to Congham, near King's Lynn, where he was holding his stag party. A mutual friend, John Bucher, drove up to Swaffham and we all set off in the car – Martin in the back and John by my side. When I accelerated after leaving Swaffham, all the loose change shot out of John's pocket. "What the bloody hell is this car?" he asked. I told him it was a BMW. He bought one very soon after and stuck with the brand for something like 30 years.

--- ooo ---

By 1974, Sadie and I were very well settled at Holmwood House, enjoying a very comfortable lifestyle there and in its beautiful grounds. Paul and James were boarders at Taverham Hall, just outside Norwich, and my third son, Michael, was attending the convent in Swaffham where his elder brothers had enjoyed an excellent grounding in their education.

A couple of years before, we had purchased a farmhouse in the village of Hunston, near Walsham-le-Willows, a few miles from Bury St Edmunds. The thinking behind this was threefold. The pressure of running a highly successful business made the prospect of being able to escape to a weekend home very appealing, even if it was only an hour away. The building needed complete renovation, and I liked the idea of having a project to manage. And we were hoping that the boys would eventually go to Culford School, which would give us yet another excuse for visiting Bury.

As you'll remember, my father was killed in World War II. I was only six and a half years old at the time and, like many of my generation, wasn't really conscious of the staggering number of deaths that occurred in that conflict, let alone those of the First

World War. But these days, I am. Wherever I am on Remembrance Sunday, I try to attend a service.

A few years ago, I recall attending one such event in Burnham Market. As with many such services, a list of those who had fallen in the wars was read out. There are five parishes in the Burnhams, and the list from each was read separately. By the time it got to Burnham Overy Staithe, where we had a house, I started to count the number there who had been killed. Those who know the village will know that, if you discount the number of properties built since, it must only have consisted of a handful of cottages and a couple of pubs when the Second World War was on. Even if the properties had been occupied by quite large families, which wouldn't have been unusual at the time, the population couldn't have amounted to many more than a hundred. Of these, something like 25 were killed.

The first loss of life from among my somewhat greater number of friends and acquaintances occurred on 3 March 1974. A few days before – on 25 February – Sadie had organised a dinner party at Holmwood. The guests were all from Bury – David and Thelma Howes, Michael and Pearl Underwood, and Bryan and Sue Ellis. Sadie provided a wonderful meal, as usual, and we all had a very happy evening. Over coffee, Bryan mentioned the rugby match in Paris the next weekend, where England would be playing France. He had a spare ticket and asked if I would like to go. I told him I would let him know the next day. Although I enjoy rugby, it was hockey I enjoyed most so, when we got to bed, Sadie asked "Do you really want to go?" I rang Bryan the next morning and declined his kind offer.

Sunday 3 March is frozen in my mind. Forty years on, I can still remember ITN's Reginald Bosanquet, with his toupee slightly adrift, delivering the six o'clock news. The headline story was about an air crash just outside Paris in which over three hundred were thought to have died, including "a group from Bury St Edmunds Rugby Club." My first thought was who could I phone? I knew David Howes wasn't going on the trip, so I rang him. Almost before I could say anything, he confirmed what I had feared. "They have all gone," he said.

That Sunday night, neither Sadie nor I slept. At that time, we weren't certain who, other than Bryan, had died. By the next morning, it was clear. Eighteen members of Bury St Edmunds club perished, including four very good friends: Brian Arthur, David Cowell, Bryan Ellis and Peter Withers.

Rising early on the Monday, we wanted to be close to Bury, so we drove down to the farmhouse at Hunston, which was habitable, but not finished. It had a large area of garden in front which had one or two trees, but was otherwise pretty bare. Feeling unbelievably fortunate not to have accepted Bryan's offer to go on the trip, I drove to Barcocks Nursery at Drinkstone and ordered a load of trees to plant in my friends' memory. After they were delivered that afternoon, I spent a couple of days with the local farm manager, planting them in an L-shape fronting the Badwell Ash and Langham Roads. Whenever I drive through the village, I look out for them. I am pleased to say that they all flourished and now form a very substantial belt of trees.

The details of the crash were recorded in a very good book called *Destination Disaster*, compiled by a team at *The Sunday*

Times. It gives a fascinating history of the growth of passenger aircraft, from the Second World War to the time of the crash but, when I first read it, it made me very angry. Like so many incidents, the crash in Paris could have been avoided. In the early days of jumbo jets, there were three competing models – the Boeing 747, the Lockheed Tri-Star and the McDonnell Douglas DC10. The 747 dominated sales in the late 1960s and early 1970s – so much so that the Tri-Star and DC10 struggled to keep up. The first division of airlines had nearly all gone Boeing, leaving the DC10 trailing third.

Lockheed and McDonnell Douglas mounted a desperate campaign to sell planes to undecided second- and, indeed, third-division airlines and they, like the airlines themselves, had cut corners to compete. In the case of the Turkish Airlines DC10 carrying my friends, the cuts had hit training. Six months before the accident, the plane's pilots had been flying single-seater jets so, when things started to go wrong, the lack of training mattered. Unlike the 747, which had dual hydraulic systems, one under the floor of the aircraft and one running above the cabin, the DC10 only had one, which, I gather, made it inherently less safe. Indeed, a 747 had previously been badly damaged when it hit the lights on stanchions at the end of a runway, ripping out part of the underside of the plane, including the hydraulics. But because it had a backup system, it was landed safely.

You might wonder why the party from the rugby club was on a Turkish Airlines' plane in the first place. But for the fact that BEA staff had gone on strike, they wouldn't have been. The only way they could get home after the match was to join a flight from Turkey to London that had spare seats on its last leg from Paris.

If you'll pardon the expression, the final nail was hammered into the coffin by the illiterate Algerian baggage handler who failed to fasten the cargo door of the DC10 properly. Shortly after take-off, it blew off, causing the cabin to decompress and taking out all the hydraulics under the floor.

A happy sequel to this sad day is that Sadie and I were responsible for introducing Sue Ellis to her second husband, Malcolm Whitley. We were pleased to offer our garden at Holmwood for the reception with family and close friends. Sue's son, Gordon, who is now a successful commercial agent in Bury St Edmunds, was very upset when Malcolm was thrown into our swimming pool.

--- ooo ---

Apart from the very personal memories of 1974, the business achieved some notable milestones. The recession was well and truly underway but, thanks to a sound business plan and prudent budgeting, we were still doing pretty well. Others weren't!

In spring of 1974, we virtually doubled the size of the firm. An architect-turned-developer, Ted Savoury from Watton, had opened estate agency offices in Attleborough, Thetford and Watton. I think his plan was to save fees on selling his own properties – rather like another businessman I knew, who bought a chain of garages so he could get cars at cost price!

I knew Ted's agencies were struggling so I wasn't surprised when, one day, I received a telephone call from him in which he told me that part of his business was taking up too much "executive time," and wondered if I would be interested. I talked to the partners and we decided that, while we were interested in the Watton office, we weren't so sure about those in Attleborough and Thetford. The figures Ted provided weren't very exciting, but I felt the offices could be turned round, enabling us to penetrate further into South Norfolk. Our existing offices were in the other parts of the county.

I can't remember the final details of the deal but, while Ted dressed it up as the "business deal of the year," it really amounted to us taking over the leases on the three offices, the hire purchase agreements on three cars and some office furniture on a similar arrangement. We also had the "honour" of being appointed sole agents for his developments. On the day the deal was finalised, solicitors from each side were summoned to his office, just outside Watton, where, after about ten minutes, Ted said he thought we could leave it to the professionals. He and I went for a ride in his helicopter!

The announcement of our takeover of the offices, which had until then been known as The Thetford Property Centre, appeared in the *Eastern Daily Press* on 29 March 1974.

Within a few days, I had a telephone call from Christopher Stone, a chartered surveyor, who was a sole practitioner with an office in Dereham. He asked if we would be interested in acquiring his business. Chris Nash, who, by this time, was playing hockey for Dereham and living nearby, was particularly keen that we should open an office there. We met with Christopher, who had an office in a prominent shopping precinct, but not much of a business. We quickly negotiated an arrangement whereby we would take over the lease of his business but allow him to stay on for what, I think, was a year. His skills were more in the commercial than residential field, so the arrangement suited both of us.

By the time we announced the acquisition on 3 May, 1974, Bedfords had grown from five offices to nine in a matter of weeks. Chris Nash immediately took over and, over the next few years, developed the office into one of the most successful in our group.

We had appointed John Deans as a partner by then, but he seemed to be developing a bit of a chip on his shoulder.

Otherwise, the firm's infrastructure was sound. The accounts and administration for all the offices were dealt with in Swaffham. Sale particulars were also prepared there, and "For Sale" boards were constructed, delivered and erected from the barn we had converted at The Hollies. Providing we had the right people securing instructions and selling property, the business could grow without causing too much disruption.

The Hollies, 1972.

Chapter 14

Shooting

I have to thank Sadie for introducing me to a hobby that has given me great pleasure for many years. It wasn't long after we moved into Holmwood when she told me, in no uncertain terms, that I needed something that would take me away from the business from time to time. Unbeknown to me, she had talked to a local farmer called Trevor Mean, the son-in-law of a farmer at Necton who had quite a large acreage and a renowned shoot. Trevor turned up one evening and announced that he had arranged some shooting lessons for me with a local chap, David Dixon, who until recently had been the clay pigeon number one shot in the country. He came round several times over a few weeks so I could practise using a borrowed gun and a clay pigeon trap that he provided.

Just after Christmas, in the last month of the shooting season, Trevor said that his father-in-law, Eddie Spratt, had invited me to join a shoot, not with a gun, but to spend the day understanding the etiquette and safety elements of shooting. I found it fascinating. The following week, I was invited again, and I was equally enthralled. On the third drive, I was standing with Trevor's brother-in-law, John Spratt, near a wood adjoining Trevor's house. When the drive began, he suddenly handed me his gun and said "Come on, you have a go." I raised the gun, pulled the trigger and down came a cock pheasant. Easy, I thought, but when I was offered the gun on a couple more drives that day, I didn't connect with any more birds. It dawned on me that perhaps it wasn't quite so easy after all.

Fired with enthusiasm, David Dixon took me to Woods, a gun shop owned by Paddy Woods, who lived at Carbrooke, near Watton. There I purchased my first gun – a Webley & Scott 12-bore with side-by-side barrels – and my own clay trap.

Over that summer, I became a reasonably good shot. When the season commenced in the autumn, I was lucky enough to be invited on several shoots and to join a syndicate that shot every Friday at Cressingham, near Watton. The syndicate's members included Noel Abel (who by this time had become a good friend), Ted Savoury, Ken Wall (the builder), Robert Crawford (a local farmer) and a jeweller from Norwich. Some of the members either had a gun-and-a-half or two guns, so they could invite guests. I met a variety of interesting people as a result. I only bought one gun, though. I couldn't shoot every Friday and neither could Noel Abel, so we had an excellent arrangement where some weeks when I couldn't go, he would take a guest and vice versa.

Range Rovers were all the vogue at the time, and several of the guns had acquired them. The guns used to get from drive-to-drive using their own vehicles, but my BMW clearly wasn't up to the task. Fortunately, Sadie had a Renault 4 that had a suitably high ground clearance and front-wheel drive, so I took that to shoots instead. To start with, the Range Rover brigade would go over the most rugged ground, through streams and down rutted muddy tracks in an attempt to shake me off, but the Renault 4 kept up with them. After a week or two, they all came to admire the vehicle ... and wonder why they had spent more than five times as much on a Range Rover!

--- ooo ---

During this period, Noel Abel ran both a sale room and a rather large removal business. He also had an estate agency with offices in Watton and Swaffham. Every Friday, he would arrive and regale me with tales of the incompetence of the staff that were running them. Over a late lunch following a shoot one day, I said to Noel "I don't know why you bother" to which he replied "Nor do I." In October 1976 – the month that marked the tenth anniversary of Bedfords' founding – we agreed to take over Noel's Swaffham and Watton estate agency offices and, in return, to divert any opportunities for furniture and removal business to him. We had run one or two auctions of property and furniture, but that side of our business didn't amount to much, so it wasn't very difficult to agree to give it up.

Under Harry Hill's guidance, the King's Lynn office had already established a sub-office in Gaywood – the area in which Sadie and I had met – and that had proved quite successful. The office in Swaffham we acquired from Noel provided us with a presence in the market square and, more importantly, a very good agency arrangement with Abbey National Building Society. We were already agents for Leeds Permanent Building Society at The Hollies. Noel's office in Watton was next to his sale room and, while it was less important to us, we did keep it going for a year or two to consolidate the connection with his business.

Noel also had extremely useful connections with all the liquidators in Norfolk and would hold regular sales of property and equipment from firms that got into trouble. One such firm was very close to home. I knew that Ted Savoury's company, Modus Developments, was struggling, but not how much. All became clear at a shoot one Friday when it was pouring with rain. We had assembled as usual and were sheltering in a barn, trying to decide what to do. In the end, we postponed the shoot until the following day. It was the only time I ever recall us doing this. While we were making the decision, Ted, bless him, in his usual manner, explained that time was money. He couldn't possibly hang around if we weren't going to shoot, as he needed to get back to the office. Noel, who was standing next to me, showed me a key in the palm of his hand and whispered out of the side of his mouth "He may go back to the office, but he won't get in. We changed the locks last night for the receiver!" Despite this, every Friday, Ted still drove his gleaming Range Rover past the shopkeepers on Watton High Street to whom he owed money, with an immaculate labrador sitting beside him and a pair of Purdy guns on the back seat. At that time, the guns were probably worth the equivalent of a couple of houses in Watton! Being a very down-to-earth and sensible chap, Noel pleaded with him to show a bit of humility, sell the Range Rover and buy a Renault "like David's." Sadly, he didn't get it.

--- ooo ---

Ted was an interesting character from a humble background. Although unqualified, he became a very successful architect/designer and built several businesses. He was passionate about motor racing and, at one stage, had his own "Team Modus" to promote Modus Developments. But he was a real Jekyll & Hyde character. He was friendly with Graham Hill, the legendary racing driver, one of whose protégés – an up-and-coming driver called Tony Brise – drove for Ted at several meetings and was guest of honour at the opening of a restaurant Ted had in Watton.

At the end of November 1975, Ted invited Sadie and me to join him and his wife Marie on a trip for dinner at the Fox & Goose in Fressingfield, the owner of which had reached celebrity status by throwing a customer's meal out of the window when he or she asked for salt and pepper! It was arranged that we would drive to Watton, and that Ted would take us on to Fressingfield in his recently acquired Rolls Royce. A couple of days before this was due to happen, we heard that Graham Hill and four others, including Tony Brise, had been killed in an air crash while returning from testing in the south of France. Ted was understandably upset by this. Arriving at his house on the way to Fressingfield, Sadie and I were invited into his sitting room for a drink. On the mantelpiece, there was a solitary Christmas card from Graham Hill and his wife, which compounded his grief. When we got home, Sadie told me she was surprised how early the Christmas card had arrived. I had already decided that it was the previous year's card, hastily retrieved for our benefit.

Ted formed other companies with varying degrees of success but, by 1986, had become a broken man. Early in 1987, he asked me to call. At that time, he was living in The Old Rectory at Cockley Cley. I had just acquired a new BMW 7 series and, when he opened the door, he looked over my shoulder and remarked what a lovely car it was. I can't remember what he was currently running, but in his heyday he drove Jensens, Ferraris and all sorts of other exotic machinery. Rather embarrassed, I wished I had gone in Sadie's car instead. Ted's last company had just gone into liquidation. I tried to talk him into downsizing and buying a modest cottage in another district, assuring him that I thought he would bounce back, but a couple of weeks later, he took his own life.

--- ooo ---

Over the years, I have been lucky to be invited to shoot on friends' farms, where the "bag" has usually finished up somewhere between 150 and 200 birds. My sister also had a wonderful shoot on her farm near Fakenham, in North Norfolk, where her husband, Martin Goodley, invited me before his untimely death. He contracted cancer at the very young age of 42. I have continued to enjoy wonderful days at Barsham and, for some time, have taken a day there so I can invite Suffolk friends to shoot with me.

In the 1970s and early 1980s, when I shot much more than in recent years, Sadie and other wives would sometimes come with my friends and me so we could make it a two- or three-day trip. We went to Lake Vyrnwy in Wales, to Yorkshire and to Scotland, where we shot grouse with Kevin Bowes and a dear friend who is no longer with us, Brian Cross. A local entrepreneur, Brian was best known for his Big Fry chain of fish and chip shops, but he was also successful in the property business.

I remember a "boys" trip to Yorkshire for a week's grouse shooting. The first half of the week went well, but it rained from the Thursday onwards. When you're shooting grouse, you spend a lot of time sitting in what is called a butt while an army of beaters walk over a mountain range or two to drive the birds towards you. Having shivered for about an hour, Brian, who was in the adjoining butt, strolled over to me and came out with a classic line "You realise what we're paying for this. We could be in Park Lane with women crawling all over us!" The day didn't improve and, in the afternoon, he visited me again. That time he told me that he had just seen "quite a good-looking sheep go past my butt!"

We were staying in a hotel just outside Leeds and, one evening, had decided to go into Leeds, where we finished up in what I can only describe as an industrial-sized dance hall. These days, I imagine it would be called a disco or nightclub. Tuesday was clearly girls' night out, and it was full of twenty-something-year-olds dancing together. I don't think teenagers were allowed out then. The nine of us were about the only blokes there. We took refuge in the bar, but were dragged onto the dance floor occasionally. In view of Brian's remarks, perhaps he was regretting not having taken advantage of what had possibly been available on the Tuesday night. To this day, when I hear Abba's *Dancing Queen*, I think of Brian and Leeds.

Another memory of Brian was when Bedfords had not been at The Hollies long and my secretary came through and said he wanted to see me in the front office. What he actually wanted was for me to go into the car park so he could show his latest acquisition off to me. It was a bright red E-Type Jaguar Drop Head. Brian insisted on taking me for a spin. It was a lovely summer's day and, with the hood down and The Eagles blaring out of the "state-of-the-art" eight-track tape machine, we drove to Mundford and back. It was all very Brian.

Sadly, Brian died in 2006. I knew he hadn't been well, but had telephoned him a few weeks before to say how much I hoped he could come to a party I had arranged to celebrate forty years in business. He said he would come if he could, but that he was having some final treatment the following week, so he might not make it. As Brian put it, if it didn't work, he was "fucked." It turned out he was right. A few days before the celebration at Burnham, Brian died. I joined hundreds of his friends and colleagues for his funeral in the church at East Dereham. One of his last wishes was that his remaining fish and chip shop in Dereham – it had also been his first – should be closed "unless my funeral's on a Friday." They don't make them like that any more!

--- oOo ---

Trevor Mean, who introduced me to shooting, also introduced me to fishing, another sport I've enjoyed for many years.

Shortly after I'd taken up shooting in the mid-1970s, Trevor invited Sadie and me to join a party fishing on Scotland's River

Tay. Before leaving, he lent me a rod so I could practise some elementary casting on the lawn at home. When we got to the Tay, I was provided with waders and a rod. Suitably equipped, I promptly stumbled and fell in. Fortunately, there was a ghillie nearby to rescue me. Dragging me onto the bank, he told me that he thought that, as it was my first trip, it would be a good idea for me to fish from a boat, rather than try wading again in the river. On the second or third day, I caught what I remember as being a 12 pound (5.4kg) salmon. Much as I had done after bagging my first pheasant, I foolishly thought "this is easy!"

During the 1970s and 1980s, I enjoyed regular trips to Scotland, particularly to the rivers Spey, Tweed and Beauly. I have a lot of very happy memories of those trips, and a few sad ones as well.

For many years, I bought my BMWs from Peter Buck, who had the franchise for King's Lynn and West Norfolk. A keen fisherman, his young son, James, would accompany us on our days out. Sadly, James developed leukaemia. I remember we were fishing the Orton Beat on the River Spey, staying in a wonderful lodge nearby. James, who by this time was receiving intensive chemotherapy, was not well, but he insisted on fishing with us and was rewarded with several salmon.

Over the years, I've enjoyed many fishing trips with Peter, including several to the Upper Floors beat on the River Tweed. The team there included the actor, Geoffrey Palmer, who, needless to say, was great company.

Peter and I also took a memorable trip to Ireland. The fishing there wasn't brilliant, but we stayed in a lovely country house hotel. All the guests were fishermen and meals were taken at one huge table. Among those staying at the time was Timothy Dalton, who was 007 in a couple of Bond films. Unlike Geoffrey, he thought he was terribly important.

One day, Peter and I decided to play golf and drove to Connemara, the most westerly point in Ireland. It was a beautiful sunny day and the views were spectacular. After signing in at the pro shop and borrowing some clubs, a lovely Irish guy in the shop pointed in a Westerly direction and told me that, with a decent drive and a good three wood, your ball would end up in New York City.

In more recent times, a party of about ten of us have enjoyed a wonderful week each year on the Spey, staying on the Ballindalloch Estate. The party has included Chris Compson, Mervin Gribbon, my son James and, sometimes, various other friends. We were very happy with the location and standard of the lodge, which sat high above the river, within walking distance of the fishing hut. The housekeeper was a lady called Diana, who we got to know very well. After showing us over the lodge on our first trip, she asked if we would like to meet the ghillie. It turned out he was her husband. When I asked his name, she replied "Dennis on a good day."!!!

Although the fishing wasn't brilliant, we visited every year until 2014. When we arrived that year, we saw that some work had been carried out on the house. Diana broke the news that the owners, the Lady Laird Clare Russell and her husband Oliver, were handing over the estate to the next generation. Clare, who is Lord Lieutenant of Banffshire, would usually invite us and any other parties fishing on the estate to the castle for a drink on a Thursday evening. This time, she asked if we were enjoying our stay and if everything was in order, to which I replied "No" tongue in cheek: I thought it was a pretty poor show that she was moving into "our house" without consulting us!

Another attraction of Ballindalloch was Oliver's pride and joy – a nine-hole golf course he had created. It was unusual inasmuch as, while having nine holes, it had 18 tees. On the second nine, the holes were approached from a different tee. It was great fun!

Chapter 15

Clouds on the Horizon

As you'll have spotted, the 1970s were a very significant time, not just for my career, but at home.

With the acquisition of The Thetford Property Centre, Christopher Stone's business in Dereham, and Noel Abel's offices in Swaffham and Watton, the firm had expanded very quickly, but I now had five partners to help – Chris Pointon, Brian Paton, Harry Hill, Chris Nash and John Deans.

I wasn't yet 40, but most people would say I was "living the dream." We had a beautiful home in a wonderful garden, our two elder boys were at boarding school, I had an up-to-date BMW, I regularly went shooting in the winter, and Sadie and I had some very good holidays – in Scotland, which we continue to enjoy to the present day, in France and in Portugal.

But not everyone thought this was admirable. As a good friend pointed out once, "I had committed the crime of being successful in a small town." The result was a number of quite unpleasant, and needless to say anonymous, letters and telephone calls.

Both the partners and Bedfords' team of managers – it included David Fletcher, Steve Marriot and Stephen Hall – were working hard and the firm was prospering, but I was providing most of the capital needed. This started to cause some friction. At a partners' meeting, somebody suggested we open an office in another town, and my response was "Fine, but where's the capital coming from? Would any of you like to re-mortgage your house?" Every one of the partners was earning a good income, taking money out of the business while leaving enough in the firm to cover tax and so on, but none had really built up much by way of capital.

Around this period, John Deans became increasingly difficult to handle. I referred earlier to the fact that I studied in the hope of gaining the auctioneers and estate agents qualifications. Although I didn't pass the exams, I maintain that I learnt more by failing them three times! Harry, Brian and the two Christophers were all chartered surveyors, so John and I were the only "unqualified" partners. John seemed to have a problem with this. Inevitably, I was spending less time at the "coalface" of the business and more behind the scenes on administration and operations. I was enjoying the pleasant duty of representing the firm at various functions but, with an increasing amount of legislation coming onto the statute books, I also had to attend a growing number of seminars and meetings. These generally seemed to be a waste of my time, but there is one thing that stuck in my mind. At a meeting in Norwich where the speaker was talking about promoting business, the message was "You never get a second opportunity to create a first impression." It's a point I've made to others many times since.

As I explained, my business started out selling retirement bungalows and other modest properties. By the mid-1970s, it was much broader-based. We were selling a lot of what, today, would be called mid-market properties but, even towards the end of the decade, the bulk of properties sold for less than £30,000. I felt that, given the area we covered – the whole of Norfolk west of Norwich – there was an opportunity for us to act for the owners of the larger houses in the area, the majority of whom were dealing with Savills at the time. I didn't think they were getting a particularly good service.

My opportunity to progress this thought came in 1976, when I was telephoned by Jon Palms, who was the managing director of Mann Egertons in King's Lynn. Among other marques, they dealt in Jaguars. Jon explained that the company was moving him – I think it was to Nottingham – and that he wanted to sell his house at Northwold. It was a fine Regency building, set in parkland and approached over a long drive. After Jon and his wife Rosemary had shown me around, I confirmed that I would be very keen to help and would give them some advice on a selling price over the next day or two, after I had obtained all the details I needed and checked the prices of comparable properties. I returned the following day to deliver my report by hand. I remember the figure was £120,000 – more than three times our average selling price. Jon said he was of a mind to instruct me to sell the property, but that he had also spoken to Savills. Aware of their policy of charging for everything, including "For Sale" boards, I offered to include all those "extras" and place a complimentary advertisement in *Country Life*. He liked my offer, but had one condition. In the case of some of the better properties we sold, I would park my BMW to one side of building so the distinctive kidney grill appeared at the side of the photograph. As the main agent for Jaguar, he asked if I would park my car behind the house before I took the photograph. I was happy to agree to this.

On my return to the office, I told Christine MacDonald about the deal. A very good secretary, she also had experience in sales. I told her that, while we wouldn't be opening a new office, we would be creating a "country house department" within the Swaffham office and I wanted her to help me with it.

We made a huge splash about The Grange at Northwold, including some large advertisements in local and regional publications, a glossy brochure and, of course, the advertisement in *Country Life*. This generated a lot of interest, and eventually a sale. The house was purchased by Malcolm and Sue Whitley, who had a joint family of six children. The happy outcome for them was a new beginning for me. I threw myself into the new venture, which very quickly took off. Within a year, we were being instructed on a nice selection of country houses – old rectories, nice farmhouses and other individual properties. Bedfords was taking a quarter-page in *Country Life* each week and I was really enjoying being back at the coalface.

When Sadie and I moved back to Suffolk some five years later, country houses and similar properties were to be the cornerstone of Bedfords' new business.

--- ooo ---

Having opened the new department, I was very busy again at work. On top of this, Sadie and I led a pretty hectic social life. Paul and James were away at boarding school and we were planning to

send Michael to Old Buckenham Hall in Suffolk in the autumn of
1977.

I had so much on my hands that I didn't appreciate how
difficult Sadie was finding things. I thought she was enjoying a
nice lifestyle, but her perspective was rather different to mine.
She thought her husband was "married to the business" and, with
her youngest son about to leave home, she was feeling
increasingly isolated.

I am the first to admit that I have always been a bit of a flirt,
and this brought things to a head in the first week of June 1977. It
was the weekend of the Silver Jubilee celebrations and the Rotary
Club was holding a barn dance and barbecue. I probably had one
dance too many with a recently divorced friend who was there
with another couple. On the way home in the car, Sadie made it
abundantly clear that she was very unhappy and even suggested
that there was no future for us. Fortunately, no-one became
aware of our problems other than our very good friends, Tim and
Mieneke, in whom Sadie had confided, and Martin and Sue Laing,
who were a great support to me. With their help, our marriage
survived. This all happened within a couple of weeks of my 40th
birthday, so I certainly had a mid-life crisis! But I realised there
were more important things in life than what had become my
"mistress" – the business. Shocked by my near miss, I lost interest
in the business for a while.

In the autumn, I had a visitor who reignited my enthusiasm.
An entrepreneur from Preston in Lancashire called Robin Savory
had spotted a niche and was in the process of developing a new
business – one that would publish a series of property

newspapers that would eventually cover the country. Bedfords was one of the largest firms in East Anglia specialising in residential properties, and he thought it would be a great boost if we published our own monthly newspaper. I contacted the partners, who all agreed it was a good idea.

In January 1978, the first issue of *Bedford – Norfolk Property News* was published. Under the banner headline – "Over 500 properties for sale inside" – it sported a very youthful-looking picture of me and a brief history of the firm. This new venture rekindled my enthusiasm for the business and was the foundation of a new friendship. Robin and his wife often stayed with us when he attended the monthly meeting at which we sorted out the following month's issue.

After leaving school, Paul, my eldest son, went on a course and received a diploma in graphic design. He then went to Preston to work with Robin, preparing newspapers for a whole variety of agents. This proved to be very valuable experience when he later joined the firm.

--- ooo ---

The firm had now grown to such a size that, even though we had a very good in-house accountant, the work of running and controlling the firm had become an increasing worry.

The final office in, as I call them, my "empire days" came through the acquisition of another sole practitioner's business – that of Nigel Horner-Glister in Holt. Chris Pointen had spent approximately ten years with me in Swaffham, but his heart had always been in North Norfolk. He had attended Greshams School in Holt and, with a young daughter and son, was hoping to send them there when they came of age. Chris Nash had had a spell at Fakenham, but was by then running the Dereham office so, when Chris Pointen and his wife Yvonne moved, we decided he should take responsibility both for Fakenham and the new office in Holt.

The office John Dean was running in Downham Market was successful, but his increasingly bizarre behaviour at partners' meetings was causing an increasing amount of stress among the others. I am not sure what finally provoked him to leave the partnership but, one day, quite out of the blue, he told me that he was going to resign from the partnership. He wanted to be paid out by the end of the month!

John's departure caused a lot of problems which were very quickly compounded when he decided to open his own office in Swaffham. The partnership agreement he had signed included a restrictive covenant, so we decided to pursue a legal remedy, but it soon became apparent that this would take a long time, so we decided not to waste any more money on lawyers' fees. Sadly John did not trust his own shadow. His business failed, as did his marriage.

Many years later, Sadie and I were attending a concert at Blickling Hall. One of the side attractions was the opportunity to have a ride in a hot air balloon. It turned out that this was John's most recent venture. A lot of time had passed by then, so we had a friendly chat. But bygones weren't quite bygones. Afterwards, I spread the rumour that John's new business was proving very profitable because he didn't have to pay for gas. He generated enough hot air himself to inflate the balloons!

--- ooo ---

John's departure was very unsettling for everyone, not least me. For various reasons that I have touched upon, I wasn't happy in Swaffham. Most of Bedfords' offices were doing well, but the one in Thetford was struggling. Chris Pointen had moved to Holt, which left me short-handed in Swaffham, but Chris Nash, who had been joined at Dereham by the very capable Steve Marriott, offered to move to Swaffham office for a time to "sort out Deans." To make things easier for him, I offered to move the country house department to Thetford and take Christine MacDonald with me. She would manage the office there and continue to help me with the larger properties.

To complete our team, we also employed a keen local lad who I thought had a great future in sales. Called Richard Ames, he made rapid progress, so I was both surprised and disappointed when, a few months later, he handed in his notice to take a job as a car salesman at a local garage. I told him that he was making a big mistake. How wrong I was! Richard went on to become big in the motor industry, with several dealerships to his name. He also became a leading figure in the equestrian world, with his own yard. I bumped into him a year or two ago at a local Boxing Day meet. He was Master of the Suffolk Hunt by then. We had a good laugh about where it had all gone so "wrong!"

Apart from hopefully rescuing the Thetford office, I suppose I was already starting to think about building a business in Suffolk. From Thetford, I could start to promote the country house sales in that direction. With hindsight, I should have known that everyone else would see my move as running away from Swaffham and the business. When the penny dropped, I decided to return to Swaffham. The business was still doing relatively well but, with all the changes, the upward momentum had been lost. Some of the offices were struggling in the face of fresh competition.

All in, I wasn't very happy!

Leading estate agents in business link-up

TWO of the best known names in house-selling and auctioneering in the western half of Norfolk, David Bedford and Noel D. Abel, are linking up in a deal which means both firms will be able to offer a much wider public service.

David Bedford, the Swaffham-based estate agents who already have nine offices in the west of the county, are taking over Abel's estate agency offices at Market Place, Swaffham and at Watton.

In addition, the firms have entered into an agreement under which any furniture or plant will be sold through Abel's Auction Salerooms at Watton. The changes take effect from today.

Mr. David Bedford, senior partner of Bedford's, commented: "We have always held a few furniture sales, but have had the considerable disadvantage of not having our own saleroom or storage facilities.

BETTER SERVICE

"Now, through our 12 offices in nine Norfolk towns, we will be able to offer everyone a much improved service in this direction, as apart from the auction department, Mr. Abel is managing director of Abel's of Watton Ltd., a thriving removal business."

On the house selling side, the link-up will mean that the range of properties offered at Bedford's head office on London Street, Swaffham, will also be on offer at the office in the Market Place.

Bedford's desperately needed more office space to expand internal departments, and these will now be housed in space leased at Abel's premises at Norwich Road, Watton, together with the property inquiry office.

Mr. Abel, who has practised as an estate agent in Watton and Swaffham for the past 20 years on his own account, said his son, Mr. Tony Abel, was more interested in the removal, storage and shipping business, and the new association with David Bedford would be an excellent opportunity to make even further expansion in this field.

Auctioneering is a profession Mr. Abel thoroughly enjoys and for which he is well-known throughout East Anglia.

He and his partner, Mr. Mike Belham, feel this new deal will improve the turnover of both modern and antique furniture through the large network of Bedford's offices throughout central and West Norfolk.

"Like all good deals it makes sense from both sides," he said. It also cements a friendship which the two businessmen have enjoyed despite working in competition with each other in the ten years since Mr. Bedford opened his first office at Swaffham in October, 1966.

Mr. Abel was the first person to be told of his plans and since then Mr. Bedford has opened offices in King's Lynn, Downham Market, Fakenham, Hunstanton, Thetford, Attleborough and Dereham.

They looked upon the move as consolidation rather than expansion, Mr. Bedford said. They were still expansion minded, but a move such as this made more sense than moving too far from home. "We have thoughts for one or two towns, however," he added.

Abel's were recently appointed official auctioneers for the Ministry of Defence.

MR. DAVID BEDFORD (left) shakes hands with Mr. Noel Abel outside his Swaffham office.

A left and a right ...not a "shotgun marriage"!

Chapter 16

Back to Suffolk

The events of this period would have a profound effect on the remainder of my career. Over 13 years, Bedfords had grown from an office in Swaffham, staffed by myself and a secretary, to an operation with 14 offices, four partners and about 70 staff.

A few months after acquiring the last office in Holt, I called in one day and the staff clearly didn't know who I was and indeed, I knew none of them. The business was at a crossroads and, as a partnership, we had already had discussions over the future, namely whether we should expand and become a Bairstow Eves. With 30 offices, it was the largest firm in the region at the time. We had much fewer, but we were number two.

A very successful firm in Huntingdonshire called Ekins was, I thought, extremely well organised. I had got to know Victor Ekins as president of St Neots' Rowing Club when I rowed for them briefly in 1954. His son, Tony, played hockey for both England and Great Britain. Quite by coincidence, Sadie and I had bumped into him when he was on his honeymoon in the Canary Islands. I telephoned him to ask if I and a couple of partners could come across to Huntingdon and have a general chat over the future of estate agency. Harry Hill, Chris Nash and I had a very enlightening day with them. One of their partners had visited America and had pioneered the firm's move into computers. The rest of us were on what I might refer to as "electric quills" at that time! They had a very sophisticated management structure and we – Harry, in particular – came away very impressed. If Bedfords was to justify the infrastructure required to run a multi-office business, it would have to grow.

That May, Sadie and I went on holiday. On the Sunday evening after we got back, Sadie asked if I was looking forward to going back to work. I admitted that I wasn't. With the fact out in the open, I spent the next week drafting and re-drafting a paper to present to the partners. In it, I said that I was no longer enjoying working in the business. I fully understood that the firm was at a crossroads. Either it had to grow considerably, or it needed to be broken up into smaller units that would be independent but, because of their heritage, would continue to work closely together. The existing partners' responsibilities offered what I felt was a basis for the latter way forward. Harry and Brian Paton were already managing for King's Lynn, Hunstanton and Downham Market, to the west of the county. Chris Nash, who was back at Dereham by this time, could team up with Chris Pointen in Fakenham and Holt to create a logical Mid/North Norfolk group. I would keep Swaffham, Watton, Attleborough, Thetford and Brandon. Based on my time at Thetford, I had already decided that the office there didn't have a future and would probably have to close. The structure of the break-up I proposed also had the advantage that the partnership owned a freehold in each of the areas.

Having produced a final draft, I went to see David Cunningham, a well-respected solicitor in Thetford who had the advantage of being an independent third party. He hadn't acted either for the partnership as a whole or for any of the partners.

On June 3 1979, copies of my proposal were delivered to each of the partners. For several days, there was a deafening silence. Finally, Harry came to see me, expressing disappointment but, being pragmatic (he was a Yorkshireman!), he said he had been authorised by Chris Pointen and Chris Nash to negotiate a settlement. The three of them were prepared jointly to take over King's Lynn, Hunstanton, Downham Market, Fakenham, Dereham and Holt. However, Brian Paton did not feature in their plans. Harry and the two Christophers instructed Norwich solicitors to act for them. John Gethin and John Wildbur were acting for me, while David Cunningham was responsible for the orderly dissolving of the existing partnership.

Brian Paton was understandably upset at being left out, and sought separate representation as a result. A thoroughly decent guy, he had worked steadily on the professional and valuation side of the business, particularly in West Norfolk but, with the side of the business that Harry and the two Chrises were taking on already having three chartered surveyors, they neither needed nor wanted a fourth. This presented a serious stumbling block.

Bearing in mind that I had instigated the split, I had to find a solution. At the time, we still had the two offices in Swaffham – the main office at The Hollies and the office that had originally been Noel Abel's in Market Place. I thrashed out an arrangement with Brian to create a separate partnership, Bedford Paton, based at the Market Place office, to which the agencies I was retaining would funnel all their professional work.

The other major point of discussion was the use of the name Bedford by the new firms. I had proposed Hill Bedford, Bedford Pointen and so on, which I thought would be of assistance to the new firms, but Harry and his partners decided they were going to launch their new firm as Hill, Nash & Pointen. I had no problem with this, other than I had to pay £12,000 to buy my name back! Irritating at the time, it was probably the best solution all round.

Amazingly, everything – the dissolution of the existing partnership, the transfer of properties and leases, and the liquidation of the limited company we had used to provide services – was complete in about six weeks. I did my best to convince everyone it was nothing personal – we had all worked hard together and built a great business, and we could all look forward to controlling our own destinies. Announcements were made and, thanks, in particular, to Harry's guidance, our new firms continued to have good working relationships. I wanted fewer agencies and ended up with three. Harry wanted more and, eventually, grew his business to have 1,100 (of which, more later). We came out of it well.

--- ooo ---

Although I had achieved what I wanted, it was a most scary time. I spent many sleepless nights wondering if I had done the right thing. Despite all the risks, Sadie supported me. Our marriage was very much back on an even keel.

The break-up obviously had huge financial implications. I hadn't been happy with the business as it was, but there was no denying that it was successful and generating a good income for all the partners. Sadie and I were enjoying a good lifestyle in a large house, we could afford to send our three children to boarding school and we had nice holidays and all the rest of it. Yet here was I "turning off the tap."

On top of this, the costs of dissolving the partnership had been considerable. I also had to buy the freehold of the Watton office, various equipment and cars associated with the business I was taking over, and find enough capital to run the new Bedfords business. Like a lot of businessmen, I was worth a great deal of money on paper, but didn't have a lot of cash.

The first decision Sadie and I made was to sell our holiday home in Suffolk. We also sold a building plot I had bought in Brancaster Staithe a year or two before. We had intended to build a house there.

The staff that remained with me were all extremely loyal and worked very hard to ensure the new business prospered.

But very quickly, I realised that I had made a mistake. Instead of going from big to small, I had gone from big to medium. To remedy the situation, I quickly decided to close the Thetford office. The country house business had been moved back to Swaffham and the staff remaining in Thetford had only been with us a very short time. Although disappointed, they were not all that surprised to hear the news.

Although each of the other offices was making a reasonable profit, I really wanted to concentrate at Swaffham on the country houses and properties in the immediate local area, where Bedfords was still dominant. I sat down separately with Stephen

Bowles, who ran the Attleborough office, and Jason Whichlow, who ran Brandon, and offered each of them the opportunity to take over their office. They both expressed interest and we soon negotiated an arrangement that I thought was on fairly generous terms. I am pleased to say that both Stephen and Jason did well – Jason particularly so. He continued to run his own business for many years, only retiring a few years ago.

This just left the fate of the Watton office to be decided. By then, I owned the freehold there outright so, following the split in the partnership, I moved Christine there to manage the office. Working with a staff of two, she did it very well.

The Watton office had, for many years, acted as an agency for Abbey National Building Society. The office majored on the sale of retirement bungalows – mostly to people from London and the Home Counties area – so this was a very successful arrangement. As the only major London-based building society, Abbey enjoyed loyal support in that part of the world as a result. When someone bought a bungalow through the Watton office, we wrote to them on exchange of contracts explaining that we had an agency for Abbey and that we were open on Saturday mornings, when money could be deposited and withdrawn. It worked liked a dream! People would be selling a house in, say, Romford, for about £30,000, and buying a bungalow in Watton for about £8,000. On the first weekend after moving in, they would drop into the Watton office and invest the bulk of the balance with Abbey. In 1979, we accepted over £1,000,000 in investments on its behalf! The commission earned paid for the staff, so Watton proved very profitable.

--- 000 ---

Back in Swaffham, I continued to expand the country house department, relying on staff including Liz Darby and Jane Sinclair to handle the local business. The firm was soon producing a decent profit, so I was able to sleep again at night.

For the first year or so, Bedfords continued to publish a property newspaper – albeit with fewer pages – but then we upgraded it to a glossy magazine. Some pages were even in colour!

With the new business going well, thoughts about moving back to Suffolk returned. Michael had just started at Old Buckenham Hall near Lavenham when Paul Rackham, a very successful Suffolk businessman who has been a friend for many years, called me out of the blue to say that he had a property that had been on the market for some time with various agents. He wondered if I would be interested in trying to sell it. To my surprise, he told me it was the former rectory in Old Buckenham, which was next door to the school. I said I would be very pleased to have a look when we picked Michael up for half term a few days later.

The rectory was a typical Regency property, set in several acres. Having looked around, I told Paul I would be delighted to try and sell it, even though it was a bit off my patch. A couple of weeks later, a gentleman came to view a rectory we were selling in Norfolk which he thought might be suitable for a special school. On his way back, he called into Swaffham, told me it wouldn't do and asked if I had anything else. I don't think I had even produced any sales particulars for the rectory at Buckenham by then, but I mentioned it to him anyway. He said he would like to have a look, so I arranged a viewing for the following weekend. To my great surprise, he rang me on the following Monday and said it was ideal. We negotiated a figure, solicitors were instructed and the school duly opened.

I had no idea at the time how useful this would be. We had been concerned about Michael's lack of progress at Old Buckenham Hall, so we decided to take him to London to see a specialist. He told us he was dyslexic. We had a meeting with teachers at his school who, like many in the profession at the time, had no real understanding of the problem or what to do about it. They just regarded Michael as "a bit behind" and hoped he would "catch up."

Imagine my reaction when, a few days later, there was an item on the local BBC News about Mr Phillips, who had bought the rectory. Standing in front of the property, he told the interviewer that the specialist school he was opening there would be for dyslexic children! The next day, I telephoned to see if there might be a place for Michael. The school was already over-subscribed for boarders but, being very grateful to me for finding him the property, he said he would make an exception if Michael could attend as a day student. Ironically, we had just sold our farmhouse at Hunston, which would have been most convenient for the school but, even though we no idea how we would organise it, we didn't waste any time in saying we would like Michael have a place at the school.

As it happens, I knew that a property in the same village as our previous home had been on the market for some time, so I telephoned the owner and arranged to rent it for three months. I would take Michael to school on a Monday morning, Sadie would travel down to Suffolk and stay Monday to Thursday evening, and I would then collect Michael again on Friday evening. It was quite an effort, but it turned out to be well worth it. Later in the year, Michael was able to join his brothers boarding at Culford School.

--- ooo ---

The arrangement with Michael's schooling saw us spending more time in Suffolk. Sadie, in particular, seized the opportunity to catch up with many of our old friends. The new business in Norfolk was doing well again, so we decided to look for another base in Suffolk.

Amongst others, I contacted Harry Turner, a gentleman agent of the old school, who had built up a very successful business by simply placing a three-line advertisement in *The Sunday Times* every week, inviting clients to contact him for country properties. He sent me a single-sheet Gestetnered description of a property at Preston, near Lavenham in Suffolk. The details contained a paragraph inviting potential purchasers to ask for a photograph if they wanted one, so I telephoned and one was duly sent. His secretary had handwritten on the back "Please return to H J Turner & Sons, Friars Street, Sudbury." How things have changed!

The property concerned was a very interesting barn. Sadie and I quickly went to see it and made an offer that was accepted. We were about to instruct solicitors when fate intervened. I had asked Harry to delay formally the instruction until I had taken the advice of an architect on my proposals for conversion. I spoke with David Brown in Bury, who made a preliminary inspection, after which I arranged to meet him at his home in Horringer to find out what he thought. Assuring me that I would be able to do what I wanted, he told me it would cost considerably more than I had thought. I had a couple of hours to kill after meeting him, so I decided to drive through the village of Dalham, where Bidwells was advertising a farmhouse for modernisation.

As I drove into the village, Malting Farm was situated prominently at the end of the street. As it was empty, I drove up to the house, parked and walked round the garden. It was an idyllic setting and, even without going inside, I knew there and then that I needed to re-organise my life so I could live there.

I drove back to Swaffham and rang Harry Turner, apologised and withdrew my offer for the barn in Preston. That evening, I told Sadie I had seen a house that I wanted her to look at. The following day, I cancelled a couple of appointments and arranged with Bidwells for us to borrow the key, which was held in the village.

While Sadie also felt it was a wonderful house and loved its situation, it was clearly a house for permanent occupation – not a second home. It had a garden of about an acre, a paddock of a further six acres and, halfway up the drive, there were some outbuildings. I suggested that we sell our house in Swaffham and move to Dalham permanently. If we did that, I would convert the outbuildings into an office and would commute back to Swaffham two or three days a week.

Although Bidwells was a highly respected firm of land agents, other than in Cambridge, it carried out very little estate agency at that time. As in the case of Dalham, they only really sold properties for the estates they managed. When it came to selling cottages and farmhouses in Norfolk, the firm often instructed me on a joint agency basis, so I knew several of the partners there as a result.

Malting Farm was on the market with the usual Bidwells arrangement: "For sale by auction unless sold privately meanwhile." The guide price was £85,000, which was within my budget, so I contacted them and expressed my interest. I wasn't surprised to hear that quite a lot of other people were interested as well, so I offered them £90,000. They turned this down, so I increased my offer to £100,000, still without success. The following weekend, I was due to fly to Scotland on a fishing trip, so I was getting increasingly concerned that I wouldn't be able to secure the property. On the Friday before I set off, the Stock Exchange took a huge dive. I can't remember why but Bidwells was clearly rattled. By lunchtime, they had called to say that, if I could stretch to £110,000, we would have a deal. The only proviso was that I would have to sign the contract that afternoon.

The sales particulars Bidwells had provided detailed the terms and conditions which would have applied had the property been sold at auction. Sadie was out, but I rang them back very quickly and said I would go to £110,000 if they lifted the covenant that required the property to be used solely as a private dwelling. I had plans to use the outbuildings as an office. They said they would have to take their client's instructions. I said I would drive to Newmarket where their solicitors, Ruston & Lloyds, had their office in any case and meet them there at four o'clock. When I got there, the room seemed to be full of Bidwells and Ruston & Lloyds partners. They said they had authority to exchange contracts and I duly signed. After they had signed the contract as well, I explained that I was not in a position to pay them the ten percent deposit on the day and would be leaving for Scotland in the morning. One of the partners from Bidwells in the room was Peter Day. A fisherman I had met previously in Scotland, he understood my priorities and agreed to accept a post-dated cheque that I said I would honour within a maximum of ten days.

When leaving for Newmarket, I had simply waved to Sadie as I drove out of the office car park. When I got home that evening and I told her we had bought a house, I got a bit of a roasting, but I knew she was really just as pleased as I was about the deal. When I left for Scotland the next day I was a very happy man. I knew I was "going home!" The following Friday, I flew home from Aberdeen to Norwich. On the Saturday morning, my bank manager, Paul Dew, telephoned to say that he had managed to persuade his directors to grant the bridging loan I had asked for, so it would now be in order for me to proceed. I thanked him very much and said that, as I had exchanged contracts a week before, I was very much relieved!

--- ooo ---

And so Sadie and I started on what was to prove to be another very hectic period of our lives.

The plans Malcolm Whitley prepared for our new house in Dalham were quickly approved and, on his recommendation, we employed a builder from Mundford to do the work. His name was Ray Nelson. We would usually drive down to Dalham in the evening at least twice a week to keep an eye on the work as it progressed.

Businesswise, the Norfolk offices were pretty busy, and we also had to think about putting Holmwood House on the market.

To generate the funds we needed in the interim, I negotiated the sale of about 30 acres of the agricultural land that had come with the house to the tenant. He was on the local council, so I should have known he would obtain planning permission sooner than most, but hindsight is a marvellous thing. The local rugby club was anxious to move to a new site, so I sold it an area of the house's parkland.

Then, in the spring, we put Holmwood and the remaining parkland on the market. Several people came to view the property, but there wasn't a lot of interest in buying it. Committed to moving to Suffolk, I began to get concerned – so much so that the staff at the Swaffham office were soon regarding me as one of their most difficult clients!

To get around the problem, we decided to exclude two acres of land beyond the rugby club, adjoining a council estate, which I felt had some potential. A new, reduced, selling price stimulated more viewings of the house, but still no buyer.

In the end, we worked out that one of the things putting people off was the swimming pool. They either didn't want one or anticipated high running costs, so I asked my team to advertise the property without mentioning it. The following weekend, the office telephone was diverted to my home number. On the Saturday afternoon, someone rang enquiring about the house. I explained that it was my own property and that they were quite welcome to come and have a look. They didn't have a copy of the sales particulars, but I showed them over the house, which they seemed to like. Strolling round the grounds afterwards, we came through the gateway that led to the swimming pool. Seeing it, the chap's wife and family all jumped up and down in excitement. The pool clinched the deal. Talk about Murphy's law!

The renovation of Malting Farm was completed by July, and we duly moved in. The office there was also finished so I set up a desk there and started to commute back to Norfolk three or four times a week, sometimes staying overnight with my mother, who was a widow again by then. My stepfather, Chris, had died a few years before we left Swaffham.

Chapter 17

Dear Bedford

After we moved to Dalham, an increasing number of people started asking when I would be opening an office in Bury St Edmunds. Several instructed me on properties in and around the town which, despite my Norfolk base, I dealt with quite successfully.

Eventually, I decided to look for an office in Bury. A few weeks before Christmas, I called on Ernest Josling, who had a two-roomed office rented from Bankes Ashton, the local solicitors. It was a few doors from my original "home" at Rutters – 86 Guildhall Street. Mr Josling was an ex-army man and chartered surveyor, very much of the old school. On the late winter's afternoon, his office was very gloomy. The few lights I remembered must have been fitted with 40-watt bulbs, and it was freezing cold. Mr Josling was at the back of the office on a typewriter, wearing mittens. Memories of Blackfriars Chambers!

When I introduced myself, the penny started to drop. As he greeted me, he pointed up the road towards Rutters' office as if I had just walked from there. I had left the town 16 years previously! I quickly got to the point of my visit – that I was thinking about opening an office in Bury and wondered if he might be contemplating retirement. I later found out he was 73 – and still climbing in roofs to do structural surveys at the time!

To my surprise, Mr Josling said he would consider it. He was clearly impressed that I had had the courtesy to come and talk with him face-to-face. Later, I found out that he had been approached by others, but usually through third parties such as solicitors. Before we parted, Mr Josling expressed concern that I might not be doing the right thing. There were quite a few estate agents in Bury St Edmunds, so I'd have a lot of competition. I appreciated his points, but explained that the office I intended to open would be specialising in country houses and similar properties. A few days later, I received a letter in his typical style. Starting "Dear Bedford," it said he was now ready to retire and that, subject to there being no problems over the lease he held from Bankes Ashton, he would be happy to discuss the terms for a takeover of his office. I soon heard from John Hooper, then senior partner at Bankes Ashton, that the firm was prepared to let me take over the lease, which had a couple of years to run, providing the arrangement would be outside The Landlord and Tenant Act. That meant I couldn't automatically demand a new lease, which I didn't see as a problem. Happy on that front, I visited Mr Josling again. He prepared a very comprehensive list of the furniture he was prepared to sell, which included a cabinet full of ordnance sheets and two very nice library chairs that Sadie and I still have in our home. The grand total for the deal would be £3,500. Mr Josling had various matters he wanted to tie up with existing clients, so he wanted to delay completion of the arrangement until the spring. I didn't have any staff and wasn't sure how I was going to run the office anyway, so that suited me fine.

As in most small towns, the Bury St Edmunds grapevine is very active, so it was only just the New Year when I received a letter from Sue Carling, a senior property negotiator for Lacy Scott, saying that she was looking for a move and had enclosed her CV. After we met, I decided to offer her the job of manager. She came with the reputation of not taking any prisoners, but I never doubted her professionalism and efficiency. We replaced the 40-watt bulbs with 100 watt ones, installed lights in the windows and turned the heating up before opening the office in the spring. After just a few months, the business had really taken off. Some clients remembered me from my days at Rutters, others came through Sue's connections and some even came in expecting to do business with Mr Josling, not realising he had retired. He had insisted there should be no payment for goodwill, so that was a bonus to us.

We occupied a couple of rooms within Bankes Ashton's premises, which were next door to solicitors, Greene and Greene. Many of my former drinking pals were now respectable partners in these firms, and several were very supportive of my new venture.

Just before Christmas, an ashen-faced Richard Freeman, then the managing partner at Bankes Ashton, came to see me to ask "What are we going to do about the electricity?" He explained that, each quarter, Mr Josling had prepared a schedule of the number of hours that the lights and electric fires had been switched on, complete with an estimate of the number of kilowatt-hours used and a cheque. I quickly realised that it would be foolish to ask what the average quarterly payment had been.

By then, we had lights burning in the windows half the night and, even in the winter, the office was often like a sauna. The heating came from old-fashioned night storage heaters that were far from controllable, so I took time to think about it. The next day, I contacted Richard and said I thought I had a solution. I explained that, as I wasn't a chartered surveyor, I couldn't possibly do the calculations in the way they had been done previously. Instead, I asked how many partners he had. Including him, it came to 14. As a member of The Wine Society, I had recently received a copy of its Christmas brochure, in which I had spotted an interesting selection – two bottles of Claret and a chucker of cheese nicely presented in a box. I sent off for 14 and, a couple of days before Christmas, presented them to each of the partners. Electricity problem solved!

--- ooo ---

To build on the success of the Bury office, we employed a couple of more junior staff but, while Sue was carrying out quite a lot of the market appraisals and valuations, I was finding it increasingly difficult to cope with both the new business and the existing ones in Norfolk.

About ten years previously – it would have been early in the 1970s – Michael Brown, the senior partner at William H Brown at the time, had approached me regarding a takeover. The firm had a large and expanding chain of offices, and was interested in acquiring our seven or eight. I visited his office in Sleaford one weekend and had a very friendly chat about it, after which he decided he couldn't afford us!

In 1982, I wrote to him saying I had been giving further thought to what he had said in his letter all those years ago. I wondered if he might be interested in the two offices I had sole control of in Norfolk. Michael, his partner, Tony Snarey, my solicitor, John Gethin, and I had a very convivial lunch at Congham Hall near King's Lynn over which we quickly agreed a deal that involved Browns taking over Swaffham and Watton, keeping all the staff. The firm would keep me on as a consultant for a year, buy the freehold on my Swaffham office and take a lease on the office at Watton.

Having swallowed my offices, the William H Brown empire continued to grow until, eventually, it was sold to Royal Insurance. Harry Hill's empire had also continued to grow, so most of the offices Bedfords once occupied had finished up in two of the largest groups of agencies in the country.

I used to see Michael from time to time when he called in either at Burnham Market or in Bury St Edmunds. After she married a trainer from Newmarket, his daughter worked with us in Bury.

--- ooo ---

Bedfords didn't stay in the office that had been Ernest Josling's for long. The lease only had a couple of years to run, so it wasn't long before I had to find new premises. After about six months, 15 Guildhall Street came onto the market. While it enjoyed a prominent situation on the corner of Guildhall Street and Churchgate Street, it was in a very sad condition. With help from the bank, I managed to secure it. A few months later, the neighbouring building – number 16 – came up for sale. Taken together, the buildings would provide enough space for a decently-sized office, but there was a lot of work to do. The project involved huge structural alterations and a substantial amount of rebuilding, but we must have done a good job. The building work was awarded a certificate of merit by The Bury Society in 1985.

In 1984, we moved in, delighted to take advantage not only of the new premises but of the two parking spaces that came with them.

Bedfords traded at Guildhall Street until Hamptons acquired the business in the autumn of 1987. As part of the deal with them – of which more later – I kept ownership of the freehold there. I used some of the money I got from Hamptons to buy numbers 18 and 19, which were just around the corner and had a large yard and buildings at the rear. More by luck than judgment, I bought the main buildings in Sadie's and my joint names and the yard and the rear building in the name of a company we had set up called Foffum Developments. This proved fortuitous, as I will reveal later.

Within a few months of taking over, Hamptons, which had grand plans for expansion and new departments, decided to seek larger premises. The buildings Sadie and I owned in Guildhall Street looked ideal so, to avoid any conflict of interest, I asked Matthew Fullerton to deal with the lease on our behalves.

Hamptons signed a 21-year lease at a substantial rent and moved in. As part of the arrangement, I released them from the lease on 15 Guildhall Street, which I was able to let to an interior designer. Again, more on this later.

When Hamptons closed its office in Bury a few years later, the lease was assigned to Bidwells who, after several years, sub-let the property to tenants including Bury St Edmunds Town Council. When the lease ran out and the tenants departed, Sadie and I obtained planning permission to convert numbers 18 and 19 into a fine townhouse and erect a new dwelling in the yard behind.

Chapter 18

Happy Times – Briefly

Having moved back to Suffolk and disposed of the remainder of my Norfolk business, I was extremely happy with my one office in Bury St Edmunds, concentrating on individual and country properties.

Despite the Falklands War in 1982, inflation running at 8.6 percent and the bank rate being at ten percent, business was good. The average house price at that time was around £25,000, but our average selling price was something like twice that.

Paul had left Culford and had joined Robin Savory, the publisher of our property newspaper, in Lancashire. Part of his job was dealing with estate agents in the North-West, and he soon learnt what a difficult breed they were! James had also left school and had worked for six months with Christine MacDonald at the Watton office before I sold it to William H Brown. James was always keen to work in the business, but I explained to him that, rather than continue to work for me, it would be good for him get experience elsewhere. He had interviews with firms including Reeds Rains in Wilmslow, Cheshire, and Earl & Lawrence in Lincolnshire, which he joined. While there, he would occasionally come home for the weekend, on one occasion telephoning Sadie to say he would like to bring a girlfriend. I looked out of the window on the Saturday afternoon to see him walking up the drive with the friend, who was less than five feet tall and wore what looked to be a pixie's boots and hat. Rather unkindly, I told Sadie he had stolen a gnome out of someone's front garden! The friend turned out to be very pleasant, but there was more embarrassment over Sunday lunch. It turned out that she was a vegetarian. She hadn't told us, so Sadie had cooked a pheasant I had recently slaughtered. We didn't see her again!

--- ooo ---

As the business started to flourish, people began to ask me if I would support local charities and good causes, which we have continued to do to this day.

At that time, Sadie and I particularly enjoyed attending concerts at the Theatre Royal, and so it was that, in March 1983, Bedfords sponsored a concert given there by Julian Lloyd-Webber. He and his brother were relatively unknown at that time.

It was around this time that Sadie and I got to know David and Ann Croft. We had met them a couple of times, but we found ourselves on the same flight from Heathrow to Portugal. They had a house there and invited us to lunch. It turned out that their daughter, Penny, was planning a TV programme about an estate agent. When we got back, she invited me to meet her.

On a gloriously sunny afternoon in the Crofts' garden in Suffolk, I did my best to explain what went on in an agent's office. Some 20 episodes of the programme – *Life Without George* – were broadcast but, despite the hints I dropped, I wasn't cast in the role!

The Crofts joined us for garden lunches and similar events over many years. At one pre-Christmas drinks party, their driver dropped them off at our house. When it was time to leave, he was summoned and a very impressive Bentley arrived, about which I made some comment. With a wicked smile on her face, Ann patted the bonnet and said "this is thanks to all the repeats of *Dad's Army*." At its peak, the original broadcasts of this, the most successful of David Croft's comedies, attracted about 18 million viewers, so I shouldn't have been surprised by the car!

A few months before David died, Ann organised a splendid 89th birthday party for him at their home near Bury St Edmunds. The dress code was described as "glamorous." It certainly was!

Sadie and I were invited to David's memorial service at St Martin in the Fields. It was an amazing production – one of which he would have been proud. A very jolly reception at the RAC Club in Pall Mall followed. Bearing in mind the fun he provided for several generations, I am sure he would have approved of this send off.

--- 000 ---

Things in my family were going well and my sister Mary – who you will recall we affectionately call Bumble – and her husband, Martin, were enjoying great success in their farming enterprises. Mother was settled in a bungalow in Swaffham, enjoying golf and painting. The sun seemed to be shining on us, but a time bomb was ticking and about to explode.

In the spring of 1983, Bumble telephoned Sadie in tears to say Martin had been diagnosed with bowel cancer. He underwent extensive treatment, including long periods at the Evelyn Nursing Home in Cambridge when Bumble would spend the weekends with us in Dalham. I would pick Martin up from the home on a Sunday morning and bring him to Dalham and Bumble would take him back there on a Sunday evening before returning to Norfolk.

Martin's great love was shooting, and he was an excellent shot. For some time, he had kindly invited me to join him on several days each season. That autumn, he managed to attend one or two shoots but, as the winter drew on, it became too much for him. Rather than cancel days, he invited me to take one or two and invite my friends. The sport was excellent, but it wasn't the most enjoyable season.

We all spent Christmas together at Bumble and Martin's home in Brancaster, but he was not at all well. I clearly remember Bill Meldrum, the head keeper at Sandringham, who Martin knew well, calling to see him and the three of us having a good natter about the previous season. They were discussing the numbers of birds they would put down for the following season, but both Bill and I knew full well that Martin wouldn't be around.

After Bill left, I had great difficulty in helping Martin upstairs to his bed. He never came downstairs again. Sadie spent a lot of time supporting Bumble after that. Early on 23 April, Bumble's birthday, she called to tell me that Martin had passed away.

--- ooo ---

One of the pleasures of shooting was seeing well-trained gun dogs retrieve and pick up the game. A few years after I started shooting in Norfolk, I happened to mention this to Sadie and we decided to look for one at the end of the season. However, on Christmas morning, Paul helped Sadie into the sitting room with a brown cardboard box that was about two feet square and tied with a large bow. He put it on the carpet by the Christmas tree, but the box didn't want to stay there. It was moving! Inside, I found a young black Labrador puppy that a local gamekeeper had been training. After making a huge fuss of it for a couple of weeks, we sent it back to the keeper, who completed its training ready for the following season in October.

I kept black Labradors for the next 30 years, sometimes having two or even three when an older dog was close to retirement. In recent years, I have only been shooting on a few days each season, but I still miss the company of a dog.

In the years when I was a more frequent shooter, Bill Meldrum used to bring a team of dogs to Martin's shoot. I've seen lots of dog handlers over the years, but nobody quite like Bill. I remember one day when we were shooting at Barsham, on a boundary defined by an old railway line. Bill positioned himself on this elevated area so he could spot any wounded birds that flew onto adjoining land. At the end of the drive, we enjoyed the spectacle of Bill controlling three dogs in three separate fields at the same time. They retrieved half a dozen birds, some of which the guns hadn't even known they had pricked!

When it was time to replace my first dog, I telephoned Bill to ask if he would be able to help. He told me that the Duke of Kent's

dog had recently had a litter, one of which should suit me. I
travelled up to Sandringham and picked the smallest of the litter. I
wasn't particularly keen on large dogs. A few weeks later, he rang
to say it was ready for collection. I asked about payment, and he
said just to bring my cheque book. I loaded Nicky, as the dog was
to be called, into the car and adjourned to Bill's cottage, where his
wife Annie had made a pot of tea. Getting out my chequebook, I
asked "Who shall I make it out to?" In his broad Scottish accent,
Bill explained that, if I made the cheque out to the estate, I would
have to add on the "VA...TEEE......"

Sometime later, when friends of ours wanted Labrador
puppies, Bill kindly agreed that a bitch I owned could be covered
by a Sandringham dog. A "honeymoon" duly took place, after
which Bill told me that the Queen's own dog, "Sandringham
Sidney," had sired Nicky. After my dog had her litter – six puppies
–I telephoned Bill to ask about the fee. He said he would let me
know. A week or so later, he rang me to say that an American oil
tycoon had been pestering him for a Sandringham dog, but the
estate had now adopted a policy of not selling puppies direct.
Instead of paying a fee, would I mind letting this chap have one of
our puppies? I readily agreed! Within ten minutes, I received a
call from Texas. I explained it would be six to eight weeks before
the puppy was ready to be picked up, and that I needed to get the
litter registered with the Kennel Club. Over the coming weeks, I
had several lengthy conversations with him, explaining that while
Her Majesty's name would be on the registration, Sandringham
could not appear as part of the name of the puppy he was
purchasing.

Eventually, I completed all the paperwork. About four weeks later, the man called me to say he was in London on business and would like to come to see the puppy. He turned up the following day with his wife and an American Airlines pet cage. I told him it was too early for the puppy to leave its mother, but he insisted on taking it. He gave me a cheque and left. Forty-eight hours later, I received a fax to confirm that he had arrived home safely. I gather that, on flights across the Atlantic, planes have specific temperature-controlled areas in their cargo holds for extra guests like dogs. The man must have been happy with this but, on the internal flight for the final leg to Texas, he bought an extra ticket – no doubt first class – so the puppy could reach its final destination! The trauma of the early weeks of his life didn't seem to affect the dog. Its new owners regularly sent us copies of the American equivalent of *The Field* that featured pictures of the dog surrounded by cups and rosettes. It had become a champion, if not of America, then certainly of Texas. Bill had advised me to charge £250 for the puppy. With the benefit of hindsight, I should have added on an extra zero!

Chapter 19

Good Morning, America!

Following Martin's funeral, I did everything I could to help Bumble. She had good friends and advisors. To her credit, she took on the farm and made a great success of it in what was – and, in many ways, still is – very much a man's world. I am sure Martin would have been very proud that his son James is now actively involved with the substantial family farming enterprise in North Norfolk.He would be equally proud with the exceptional career his daughter Kara has built with her London based PR company in the fashion world.

In the early summer of 1984, Sadie and I decided to take a long weekend break. Not having planned anything, we mentioned it to our good friend Chris Compsom. He said "Why don't you go to the South Coast and have a long weekend in Brighton?" With nothing booked, we set off. Eventually, we arrived on the promenade where, driving along, we came across The Grand Hotel. The season hadn't begun, so the town wasn't terribly busy. We strolled into the hotel and asked for a room. I can't remember how much they said it would cost, but it was only £20 extra for the grand suite, which included a television in the sitting room as well as the bedroom – the height of luxury in those days. After a lovely weekend, we returned home and didn't think much more about our stay until the autumn.

That year, the Grand Hotel hosted the Conservative Party's annual conference. It was a fateful year. The IRA planted a bomb behind the bath panel in the grand suite we had occupied just a few months before. One of the serious casualties of that dreadful event was Norman Tebbit's wife, who is confined to a wheelchair for the rest of her life. Happily, they are now enjoying their retirement living in Bury St Edmunds.

While investigating the explosion, the police at one point speculated that the bomb might have been placed in the room some months previously and detonated remotely. On that basis, I was surprised I didn't hear from them. Perhaps the register had been blown up and they had no record of our occupying the room.

--- ooo ---

1984 also saw the commencement of the miners' strike that so divided the country.

Early that year, I was invited by the National Association of Estate Agents to join a delegation that would visit the United States for three weeks the next May. We all met at Heathrow for the direct flight to Chicago. It was a long flight, not helped by the delay of two hours we had to endure sitting in the plane – a Boeing 747 – at Heathrow. We were flying economy, but the plane was by no means full, so most of us were able to stretch out over three or four seats.

We would be visiting four cities – Chicago, Dallas, Orlando and Washington DC – on our tour. Most of us thought Chicago would be of least interest. How wrong we were! We were keen to know how the American property industry worked but, after the tiring flight, we were thankful for a 10am start the following day. Suitably refreshed, we were given a general overview of the market and how it operated in the States. In the afternoon, we had a trip around the city during which our guide, a lovely middle-aged lady called Blossom, showed us the biggest and best Chicago had to offer.

The next day, we visited Coldwell Banker, the largest corporate realtor in the United States. There, we met one of their executive vice presidents. We soon learnt that, in America, most middle-ranking managers enjoyed the title of Vice President! At the time, Coldwell Banker operated on a basic 7.5 percent commission that it shared with the listing and selling agents and, usually, with the sales staff involved. We were given a very interesting insight into the workings of a large corporation, its staffing levels, the average incomes of sales staff, training and techniques and the idea of having self-employed licensed agents attached to a corporate company branch.

Some of the statistics they reeled off stuck in my mind. In 1975, Coldwell Banker's sales force had been 75 percent male but, by the time of our visit, it was 75 percent female. I wouldn't be surprised if there were even more women in the business today. We also learnt that Coldwell Banker converted approximately 50 percent of its enquiries into sales.

While in Chicago, we were also entertained by what, compared to Coldwell Banker, was a medium-size realtor –the Du Page Board. Larger than any group in the UK at the time, it was a fairly modest business by American standards. We got on extremely well with the team there, learning a lot about multi-listing and the computerised facilities that they had, even back then. Before we left, they presented each of us with a plaque bestowing honorary membership of the Board.

We also visited a practice that had recently been established by some ladies. The shop front was undistinguished, but at least it was there. None of the listings in the window included a photograph, but it felt a little more like home. Once inside, prospective purchasers were greeted by an awe-inspiring row of 15 desks – all exactly the same apart from the occupier's name plate. We learnt that realtor associates were stationed at desks on a rota that required each to put in "floor time" – usually, a three-hour period – two or three times a week. The office was open seven days a week, and associates could also be at their desks at any other time of day or evening they chose, provided they didn't take "cold enquiries," either by phone or off the street. They must be handled by the "floor" girls.

We joined members of the team on their Thursday morning round of "new listings."

Each of us paired up with a lady realtor equipped with a sales pack that included tips on preparing a house for viewings. I was fascinated to see an aerosol which apparently contained "Mama's Home Cookies." Before viewers arrived, owners of properties were instructed to give their kitchens a good spray to give the impression of freshly baked cake, and to keep their fingers crossed that nobody asked to look in the oven, which in most cases was unused! While out and about, I saw an interesting cross-section of property, ranging from a seedy four-storey building divided into eight apartments – where the usual estate agent's nightmare of the keys ensued – to a Victorian mansion that, even 30 years ago, was on the market for approximately $1.8 million. The realtor and I went on to see a charming Victorian home with a real live owner who scuttled into the back store room looking somewhat bemused when we all arrived. We then proceeded to a warehouse that had been converted into (very quiet!) shops and restaurants. It was there that we had lunch. The owner of the restaurant was the third to try his luck there, the previous two having gone bust.

One of the most interesting properties we saw was the former Dr Scholl's factory, which had just been converted into apartments. It was the first example of what most of us came to know as loft conversions – amazing spaces with their brickwork, services and air conditioning exposed and brightly coloured paintwork.

Before we left Chicago, we visited the Sears Tower which, at that time, was the tallest building in the world. The express elevator travelled to the 110th floor, some 1454ft (443m) above the ground, in less than a minute. There were the most amazing panoramic views over Chicago and the lake. Even though it was a perfectly still and sunny day, if you lined a feature of the building up with one on another skyscraper, it was clear there was still a gentle movement at the top. We subsequently found out that the design provided for a movement of up to 18ft (5.5m)!

--- ooo ---

The following day, we exchanged a sad farewell with Blossom and caught a 7am flight to Atlanta, an airport we got to know quite well, as every leg of our journey seemed to go through there. We then caught a flight to Dallas (Fort Worth) Airport, where the temperature had risen to 85°F (29°C). The guide who met us told us the airport there was bigger than that in Chicago, at which point everyone dissolved into laughter. According to Blossom, everything in Chicago was the largest in the States, if not the world!

Dallas had a spectacular skyline of relatively new skyscrapers. Among them was the head office of mortgage provider, Lomas & Nettleton, which many of us thought looked somewhat familiar. Apparently, it was where the Treasury Oil Corporation, a "star" of the TV series Dallas, had its head office, but there was no sign of JR or Bobby in the building. Lomas & Nettleton's offices started on the 36th floor and went up, but had a distinctly old-world feel. Stepping out of the lift, we were confronted with priceless English antiques, expensive tapestries and paintings, and valuable works of art. The building was barely three years old, but you felt like you were in a fine old period property.

Lomas & Nettleton's business was basically providing finance for property purchase. In the UK, the loans home-buyers need traditionally come from building societies or banks. The debts are held by the lending institution, which covers them using money raised from high-street and other depositors. Lomas & Nettleton marketed mortgages through a number of imaginative schemes, setting up systems to administer repayments and service the mortgages, then selling them on to investors – pension funds and other institutions. In theory, this left the firm free from almost all the risk and worry involved, but earning ongoing fees from the administration work. Writing this some 30 years later, it's easy to see how this system was abused. Good- and poor-quality loans were bundled up together and sold to investors who had very little idea what they were buying. In 2007, it went spectacularly wrong.

No visit to Dallas at that time would have been complete without a visit to South Fork Ranch, the place where much of *Dallas* was filmed. I must say, it was a big disappointment. It's amazing what film companies can do with aerial shots and a wide-angled lens. In the flesh, it reminded me of a chalet bungalow in a fairly dismal area, somewhere between King's Lynn and Wisbech.

--- ooo ---

We moved on to Orlando, once again via Atlanta.

Dominated by nearby Disney World, the area was very different in character, and nowhere near as affluent as Dallas or Chicago. As well as meeting realtor groups in and around the city, we visited the Epcot Centre.

The realtors introduced us to the concept of "zero-lot" developments – estates of fairly large properties, none of which had a garden. Each development was dominated by a large country club with a golf course, tennis courts and other facilities so, when it came to recreation, you could either stay indoors watching a giant television or go to the club. The worst possible place to open a garden centre!

Finally, we flew to Washington DC – again via Atlanta! While our time there included more meetings with property people, we had a fair amount of spare time to explore what I thought was a most fascinating city. Unlike others across the United States, it's far from high rise. Back in 1910, the city ruled that no building could be more than 130ft (40m) tall, so most of the buildings are just four or five storeys high. I visited the Washington Memorial and various public buildings, and paid a very moving visit to the Vietnam Memorial – a huge wall of marble with tens of thousands of names carved into it. It reminded me of the memorial at Monte Casino that bears my father's name. We never seem to learn the lesson of war.

A friend of Sue Laing – a close friend from Norfolk – was working at a hospital in Washington, so I contacted her and invited her out for a meal. Vanessa, picked me up at the hotel in her bright yellow Volkswagen Beetle and we headed off to a restaurant in Georgetown I had asked her to book. The fashionable area is packed with fine restaurants, most of which offer valet parking. Nearly all the vehicles at this particular restaurant were massive limos. A very large African American appeared to deal with the car, and I could tell by the look on his face that he didn't think we would be good for a tip. Once we were out of the car, I took the keys from Vanessa and lobbed them towards the valet, telling him in true Hollywood style to "lose it."

--- ooo ---

Over the three weeks we spent in America, conversations between the agents in the group inevitably loosened up. None of us was a competitor, so talk eventually turned to business. It soon became apparent that most of the others had had a tentative approach from one institution or other about the possibility of selling up. I hadn't had an approach at that stage, so I felt a bit left out!

The group was composed of a very interesting cross-section of personalities, many of whom either were or became well known in the profession.

The delegation leader was a Maureen Freeman, a lady who ran a small group of offices in Cardiff. She worked tirelessly for the National Association but, sadly, died a few years ago.

Sue Porter, whose south-London firm was called Taylor Dixon Porter, was accompanied by her husband. It turned out she shared a birthday with me – the date, not the year – and we still keep in touch. James, my middle son, had a spell with her firm in Putney after he left Earl & Lawrence of Lincolnshire.

Keith Egglestone ran a business in Essex called S & M Processing, which pioneered and cornered the market in self-adhesive computer labels. Up to then, agents had included rather indifferent black and white pictures in property details. Suddenly we had colour photographs on the property details, but were employing extra staff to stick them on. At the time, the Americans were light years behind us on presentation and were overwhelmed with his product. I believe he subsequently opened a base in Florida and ran a very successful American operation.

I got on very well with another couple, Iain and Valerie Hogg, who subsequently attended my 50th birthday celebrations. A partner in a thriving Glasgow agency, he sold out to the TSB not long after the trip.

Trevor Kent – a larger-than-life character – was well known, not only in the profession, but to the public at large. He often appeared in the media, trying to put the public right about property issues.

David Perkins had already been the president of the National Association and was well known throughout the profession. He took a particular interest in agency-related legislation.

Charles Smailes, who more recently became president, not only ran a very successful practice in Harrogate, but had a national reputation as an auctioneer.

Geoffrey Smushall and his wife ran a successful 20-office practice based in Leicestershire at the time. I believe they subsequently sold out to Prudential.

And finally, I remember a non-agent delegate, Derek Wilson, who was a regional manager for Abbey National Building Society. I spent quite a lot of time with him and Charles Smailes. He and his son, Danny, took over a letting agency in Bury St Edmunds that was virtually opposite Bedfords. Danny joined my local golf club, but he's a scratch golfer, so I don't get invited to play with him. Funny that!

Chapter 20

Big Bang in the City
& Estate Agency

In the mid-1980s – a time of boom and bust in the City – a great many estate agencies were taken over by banks, building societies and other corporate bodies.

Interestingly, the cradle for this "corporatisation" of the estate agency business sprung from King's Lynn in Norfolk. As you will recall, I opened my second office in 1967. Located in King's Lynn, it was managed by Harry Hill from the early 1970s until the partnership was dissolved. Our main competitor in the town and across much of West and Mid Norfolk, was Charles Hawkins & Sons. I think it was in the autumn of 1982 that I was in King's Lynn having a meeting with my solicitor, John Gethin, when our meeting was interrupted by a telephone call from his secretary. When John put down the phone, he told me that "Charles Hawkins had been taken over by Lloyds Bank." Our initial thought, which we found very difficult to believe, was that the bank had moved in and taken the firm over because it was in financial trouble. Adjourning to the bar of The Duke's Head Hotel, we found it buzzing with local agents and solicitors, including a couple of partners from Hawkins. They confirmed that Lloyds Bank had purchased their business, but told us the firm would be the basis for a national group, to be named Black Horse Agencies.

Lloyds then embarked on a succession of takeovers of firms, acquiring Januarys in Cambridge and several other very good agencies.

Around the same time, Harry and his partners had merged their business with Abbotts to form a 32-office group. Other mergers soon followed, including those with Bairstow Eves and Mann & Co. A little later, Hambros Bank took a stake in Harry Hill's business, renaming it Hambros Countrywide and listing it on the London Stock Exchange with Harry as its chief executive.

Over the next two or three years, various institutions – in particular, the Prudential, TSB and Royal Insurance, which by then owned William H Brown – joined the stampede to build up agency groups.

In 1986, the race reached Bedfords. I was approached by the Nationwide Building Society, which was looking for a vehicle to sell more mortgages and life policies. An article published at that time referred to the "world of difference" between selling estate houses and the individual marketing of period properties by specialists equipped to carry out such instructions. Negotiations with the Nationwide didn't get very far, but the indication was that they would be prepared to pay something like £500,000 for my one office. I resisted the temptation and soldiered on ... well, until 1987, at least.

--- ooo ---

Sadie and I were spending a weekend with my sister in Brancaster. On the Saturday evening, she had been invited to a drinks party by David Johnson, a farmer from The Fens who had a finger in many pies. Sadie and I were also invited to go along. With a glass in my hand, I was enjoying the view over the marshes from his splendid home when David drew me to one side and asked if I had ever thought of selling my business. I told him of my flirtation with the building society and my reasons for turning it down. He said he knew of a company that would be a much better fit for my business if I did decide to sell it. On my second or third glass by then, I said "If they would like to contact me, give them my number."

A couple of weeks later, I received a telephone call from a partner of Hamptons, a national firm with a head office in Arlington Street, opposite The Ritz Hotel, in London. Specialising in country houses, Hamptons was then owned by a company called Abaco, a wholly-owned subsidiary of the now-defunct firm, British & Commonwealth Holdings. Its chairman, John Gunn, turned out to be a great friend of David Johnson, hence the approach.

Two of Hamptons' partners – Stephen Perks and Charles Bailey – came to meet me in Dalham and told me about the firm's plans to expand in East Anglia. It had recently taken over Sworders' office in Saffron Walden, which had been run by a great character called Bruce Munro, and J M Walsh & Sons, which had offices in Great Dunmow and Thaxted, run very efficiently by Tim Trembath. They indicated that, if they acquired my business, they would be looking to expand into Norwich and, probably, into Cambridge.

I was approaching my 50th birthday and, while James was interested in the business, Paul was working for Bennetts at the time, selling new bungalows, and Michael was just about to leave school. I had long discussions with my solicitor, John Gethin, and John Wildbur, who was my accountant. Still very undecided, I told John Gethin to tell Hamptons I would think about selling my business, but wouldn't consider any offer below £1 million. I thought the amount would put them off, but it didn't! Meetings took place, including one I clearly remember in Arlington Street during which Hamptons' financial director took my accountant into an adjoining room to explain how he could adjust my accounts to apply the multiple that would enable them to offer the magic figure.

A deal was agreed in principle, but I explained that I needed a week or so to finally make up my mind. It was a few weeks before a birthday party Sadie had planned for me that involved a marquee in the garden and about 80 guests, so I arranged for us to fly to Jersey for a week's holiday, away from everything and everybody, so that Sadie and I could make a decision. The sun shone and the surroundings of Longueville Manor were wonderful. Eventually, we decided I would go for it if the contract I was offered wasn't too long and the deal was structured in the best possible way from the point of view of tax. One thinks of these things when one is enjoying a holiday in a tax haven! In anticipation of the windfall, Sadie bought a rather expensive dress for my birthday party before we flew home!

Decision made, the lawyers and accountants got to work. The two Johns and I spent several days in London at the offices of

Frere Chomley, Hamptons' solicitor, in Lincoln's Inn Fields. I clearly remember one amusing conversation with Rosemary Bott, the lady who led the team working for Hamptons. We worked through the day and had a sandwich lunch brought into the board room. During one of the breaks, I asked her if Frere Chomley specialised in anything in particular. She said "Oh yes – boundary disputes." Given the splendid offices and setting, this came as something of a surprise. I had just been involved in a £500 boundary dispute in connection with a small chicken run in Cockfield, near Lavenham. It would have taken a lot of misplaced chicken runs to keep up Frere Chomley's offices! I said "Really?" She replied "Oh yes, we do a lot of work in South America, resolving disputes between countries!"

--- ooo ---

John Gethin knew I wouldn't be happy in a corporate situation. He insisted that my contract with Hamptons should be for no more than three years, as opposed to the five they had requested. My business was doing extremely well at the time and Hamptons was anxious to benefit from it as soon as possible. They hoped for July, I think, but the deal wasn't completed until early in October. Despite the delay, John insisted that my contract should be deemed to have started in July. It was also agreed that I would maintain my office at Dalham and that Hamptons would make a contribution towards its running costs. We insisted that the sale be structured in such a manner that I would be able to take advantage of rollover relief. I subsequently discovered I was the only director around Hamptons' boardroom table to have achieved this.

Sadie and I were both partners in the business at the time, so we had to convert the partnership into a limited company before it could be sold. Hamptons would then purchase the shares. To achieve this, Sadie, John Gethin and I flew to Paris – Air France, business class of course – and stayed at The George V overnight. The following morning, we met with French lawyers and completed the first stage of the process – from partnership to limited company. When we got back to Heathrow, the owners of Hamptons, Abaco Investments, met us, purchased the company and handed over a cheque for £550,000 and shares in Abaco worth £450,000.

On 9 October 1987, I was a millionaire. The following weekend – 15 and 16 October – a great storm swept over Britain then, on what became known as Black Monday, the stock market crashed. The Abaco shares I owned were almost halved in value overnight, but recovered when British & Commonwealth absorbed the company soon afterwards. British & Commonwealth had its own problems, but after six months, when I was allowed to sell the shares, I sold them all. I have always preferred bricks and mortar to pieces of paper!

As I will explain later, I left Hamptons a few months before the end of my contract, which meant I only worked for them for about two-and-a-half years. The wisdom of having structured a deal that entitled me to rollover relief became clear but, to secure the benefit, I had to buy a qualifying asset within three years. I managed it with just a few days to spare. Eventually, I was able to reclaim the capital gains tax paid on the shares I received from Hamptons. Overall, the £1 million I had originally received for my business was more or less secured.

--- ooo ---

But back to my arrival at Hamptons...

Like the principals of the other firms the business had acquired, I got a seat on the board. I remember a lot of discussion about "products and synergy" at the time. I kept quiet, but more and more meetings were scheduled, which meant catching early trains to London and sitting through what seemed like interminable meetings, rarely getting back before late afternoon. At the third board meeting I attended, I expressed my views pretty strongly: "You don't earn any money in meetings." Bruce Munro, who travelled back with me on the train, thought I might have pushed my luck too far. Sure enough, I got a telephone call from the Chief Executive, Graham Clarke, the next day, asking if I would go up to London the following evening to see him. I mentioned this to Bruce, who wished me luck. Following the meeting, I was able to ring Bruce, thank him for his concern and tell him not to worry – I had been promoted to regional managing director and given a pay rise. Graham clearly wanted me inside the tent pissing out rather than outside pissing in! I told Bruce that I had also been given the dubious responsibility of trying to control him for the next three years!

Corporate life might not have been for me – and it wasn't – but I learnt a lot during my time with Hamptons. Previously, my business plans had been on the backs of envelopes. While I was with the firm, I quickly learnt not just about budgets, cost control, PR and marketing, but also how not to run a business. Towards the end of my days there, someone asked me how to create a successful small business. "Start with a big one," I replied!

Bury estate agency sold for £1m

AN ESTATE agency at Bury St Edmunds specialising in country house sales has been sold for a price of £1 million.

The business was established in 1982 by Mr David Bedford, and the purchaser is Abaco Investments, which has a number of estate agencies dealing in the country house market, including the West End firm of Hampton and Sons.

The Guildhall Street office of David Bedford in Bury will become part of Hamptons, East Anglia, and Mr. Bedford, 50, will be a director. He first set up as an estate agent on his own account 21 years ago.

Mr Bedford said that with the rapidly changing face of estate agency practice in the country, he had had several approaches from companies wishing to buy his business.

Mr. Bedford trained with and then was on the staff of Rutters in Bury St. Edmunds between 1957 and 1966. He then moved to Norfolk, where he set up a chain of estate agencies.

He sold out in 1980 and returned to Bury St. Edmunds, where he bought the business of the late Mr. Ernest Josling and then set up David Bedford.

In the year to 31 July, 1987, David Bedford made a pre-tax profit of £103,000 on turnover of £283,000. A total of 176 sales was completed, with an average price in excess of £90,000.

The consideration of £1 million from Abaco Investments was paid in full on completion, £550,000 in cash and £450,000 by the issue of 492,340 ordinary shares of Abaco at 91.4p.

Mr David Bedford

Sue Carling would continue to manage the office and had been appointed an associate, as had Charles Merrifield.

October 1997 – just before Black Monday!

Chapter 21

One Tea Bag or Two?

The sale of my business to Hamptons caused quite a stir, and not just in the local media. It was also reported in *The Financial Times*.

It was, of course, a very comfortable feeling to have a substantial financial buffer against whatever life might throw at me and, because I had been under no pressure to sell, the deal had been done on my terms. The millionaire tag didn't sit comfortably with me but, as I explained in the previous chapter, it didn't last very long.

To celebrate our Silver Wedding the previous year, Sadie and I had been on a trip to Kenya that included a safari. It also included a stopover at a beach resort, where I was taken ill – with food poisoning, I suspect. I took to my bed and Sadie, via the hotel, arranged for a doctor to visit. Looking out of the window an hour or two later, she said "I believe the doctor has just arrived." Well, she was pretty sure he was a doctor anyway, as he had "a bone through his nose." Worried that a witch doctor was coming to see me, I was relieved when a very competent local doctor came into the room, examined me and gave me some medication. I recovered within just a few hours.

The first leg of the flight home was to Nairobi Airport, where we boarded a Boeing 747 Jumbo Jet that that had touched down en route to London from Johannesburg. It was absolutely packed and our seats were in the middle of a group of four in the economy section. The aisle seats on either side of us were occupied by large, sweaty, African gentlemen. Those in front were fully reclined, and the lavatories were unspeakable. When we touched down at Heathrow the following morning, I told Sadie I was never ever going to fly economy on a long-haul flight again.

--- ooo ---

I soon discovered that my new role as regional managing director had very little to do with selling houses. Head office sent endless memos requiring information, some of which I managed to farm off to Sue Carling, Charles Merrifield who became associates after I sold the business. I made sure that Bury continued to out-perform many of the offices in the group, simply by telling Sue and Charles to ignore some of the memos they were sent.

Visits to Hamptons' head office in Arlington Street were, unfortunately, inescapable. To get there on time, I had to get up at about six o'clock in the morning and catch the seven o'clock train from Audley End, near Saffron Walden, to Liverpool Street. The full effects of Black Monday and the chaos that ensued didn't truly impact Britain's economy until well into 1988. A good barometer of the state of the markets was, I thought, the length of time I had to wait for taxis on my regular journeys to London. By 1990, when I stopped making them, the recession had really deepened. The taxis were queuing up for me rather than the other way around!

The first six months as an employee I found fairly difficult and exhausting so, as a surprise Christmas present for Sadie, I booked a holiday in Barbados for the February of 1988. On Christmas Day, I presented her with a small package containing a new swimsuit and the airline tickets to the island, which were business class on the way out and Concorde for the return.

People often asked me if the sale of my business to Hamptons had affected our lifestyle. Bearing in mind the pretty good one we had had beforehand, I was able to truthfully say "No," but with two exceptions. The first was that, in the future, we would fly business class on any long-haul flight, but the second was somewhat more modest. For much of our married life, I have woken up before Sadie, gone downstairs, skimmed through the papers and made each of us a cup of tea. A week or so after selling the business, I was going through the usual routine one morning – of boiling the kettle, filling two mugs with hot water, then dipping a single tea bag alternately into each mug – when I suddenly thought "What the hell am I doing messing about with one tea bag?" From that day, we have enjoyed an individual tea bag each!

--- ooo ---

During my time at Hamptons, I got to meet a lot of interesting people, many of whom I still keep in touch with. For the first six to nine months, despite Black Monday, things in London and The City seemed to carry on much as before. The East Anglian offices for which I was responsible continued to perform pretty well. She hadn't been happy with the new arrangements to start with, but Sue Carling was producing very good results in Bury St Edmunds. She clearly felt I had abandoned her, but I now had other responsibilities. Thanks to the enormous goodwill he had built up, Bruce Munro continued to perform well in Saffron Walden and Tim Trembath continued to put in good results in Great Dunmow and Thaxted.

Neither Tim nor Bruce was a company man. Tim still managed to shoot two or three days a week. I didn't have a problem with this – I simply didn't tell head office. With his contacts, Tim, in particular, brought in a lot of business. There would be a flurry of memos from head office or various departments every week but, knowing the characters, I encouraged my team to ignore them.

I was under pressure from the board to open more offices in East Anglia, the first of which would be Norwich. My accountant, John Wildbur, drew my attention to some premises in Prince of Wales Road. The road was full of agents' offices at the time but, today, it's all nightclubs! It was not a prime location, but the rent was reasonable and I convinced the board that it would get our foot in the door.

After his spell in London, my son James had been helping Bruce Munro out at Saffron Walden. Bruce suggested that he should be transferred to the new office. It made steady progress – because of my previous business, it was attracting instructions from Mid and North Norfolk, as well as from the local Norwich area – so, about nine months later, when an opportunity arose in Upper King Street, I recommended that we pursue it. The prime corner premises were between Bidwells and Savills, and virtually next door to Strutt & Parker. The rent was a very modest £12,500 a year at a time when Bidwells was paying somewhere between

£60,000 and £70,000 for the admittedly larger premises next door – but, to reflect this, the owner wanted a premium of something like £50,000. But while my team was doing well, it was becoming apparent that the majority of the group was haemorrhaging money. The scale of the problem became clear when Hamptons found itself unable to produce the money I required up-front.

This was the moment when I decided my heart was no longer in it, and I started looking towards the exit. In a meeting with Graham Clarke, I reminded him of a side letter that said I only needed to devote the "majority" of my time to Hamptons. I had worked extremely hard for two years, so I asked for two months off as a sabbatical. By coincidence, a friend called Tony Mullucks, to whom I had been introduced by Henry Pryor, had just come to the end of his contract at Prudential, so I suggested that he should be brought in to share my job as joint regional managing director. If that was acceptable, I would drop down to part-time and take a reduced salary on my return. Graham agreed to everything immediately.

Tony lived near Bishop's Stortford and we travelled up together for his first board meeting. Sue Porter, several other board members and I had established a routine of meeting in the nearby Ritz Hotel for breakfast – yes, The Ritz! – before strolling across Arlington Street for the meeting. In the taxi, I told Tony about this arrangement, which he thought was an excellent one. When we got to the Ritz, we found no-one else there, but enjoyed a very pleasant breakfast and coffee nonetheless. When we got to the board meeting, it was clearly in full swing. Nobody had told me it had been brought forward three-quarters of an hour. I used a rather school-boyish excuse – that the train had been late – but smirks around the table suggested several people knew where we had been.

Early in 1990, Sadie and I went on a six-week trip to Australia, after which I worked full-time for a few months. By the spring, I had pretty much put in enough hours to see me to the end of my contract.

One of my jobs during that period was to close the Norwich office. Hamptons' short lease was about to expire, so there wasn't much alternative, but I had recruited Tim Hayward from London to run the office, and he had moved to Norfolk with his family to take the job. Feeling very bad about this, I rang James Buxton, the senior partner at Bidwells, before announcing the closure. I knew the firm was looking for someone for its Norwich office. Subject to interview, James said he would be very happy to offer Tim a position – particularly as I indicated he might well bring 15 or 20 instructions with him! Tim enjoyed a successful time at Bidwells, but left eventually to join Jackson Stops & Staff. He has just opened an office for them in Burnham Market. There you go!

--- ooo ---

By the time I left Hamptons, Graham Clarke had moved on. British & Commonwealth was in trouble and had sold the business to the Bristol & West Building Society. I didn't like the sound of this at all! Having sold out to Hamptons and served their terms, quite a few of the original principals had departed, their places being taken by what I can only describe as middle management. They understandably had chips on their shoulders regarding people like me, but I felt I should do the right thing. Tony, Bruce Munro, Tim Trembath and I put a plan together for what, today, would be called a management buyout of the eastern region offices. For what I thought, at the time, to be all the wrong reasons, they rejected the proposition. With hindsight, I thank goodness it was declined. While we all had varying restrictions in our contracts of employment, these were all due to expire the next year.

Although I had three months left on my contract, I offered to leave without payment. I was looking forward to the challenge of starting yet again, and was far from sorry to be giving up my relatively short career as a commuter.

I hadn't always enjoyed my time at Hamptons, but I did learn a lot from the experience. The firm had carried out a lot of research as to what motivated vendors to instruct a particular agent, for example. I have never forgotten that, down in fourth place, was the fee. Far more important were the agent's perceived track record within the market sector in which it was operating and personal recommendation. Also high on the list was the quality of presentation. In the early 1990s, I don't think anyone had heard of the word website but today, of course, that is most important.

Interestingly, at the time I was working on the first draft for this chapter – the spring of 2014 – about half a dozen new agents moved into Bury St Edmunds over just a few months. The majority were existing businesses moving from nearby towns where they hadn't enjoyed particular success. I later discovered that some of the firms had no idea that others would be opening nearby! With nothing in particular to differentiate themselves from competitors, the only option was to reduce their fees. As Hamptons' research showed, this doesn't work. Agents attracted just what they didn't want: overpriced properties that had been on the market for some time.

--- ooo ---

With the benefit of hindsight, I suppose 1991 could be regarded as "half time" in Bedfords' history.

Over the first 25 years, I first made the firm a major player in Norfolk, then reinvented it as the niche business that I eventually sold to Hamptons.

After I left Hamptons, Sadie and I had long discussions as to whether I should start another business or not. Friends told me that, with a million in the bank, I could retire but, while we were financially comfortable, I couldn't imagine never working again. I was only in my early fifties, after all!

The most important consideration was, of course, our sons : Paul, James and Michael. If I was to launch "Bedfords Mk 3," we thought one of them might be interested in carrying the business on, so that's what I eventually decided to do. I promised Sadie that I would only be involved for a "year or two," but it didn't quite work out like that.

--- ooo ---

Having decided to relaunch the business, the first question was how. When I left Hamptons, it was with a restrictive covenant that meant I couldn't open an office in Bury St Edmunds before February 1991. But while Dalham is close to the town, it isn't Bury St Edmunds, so James and I laid plans to use the office at our home in the village.

Once we were operating very successfully from our "rural shed," we thought again about opening an office in Bury St Edmunds. Talking to my accountant, the decision was clear. To recoup the capital gains I had paid, I needed to buy what's called a "qualifying asset" – another property. The clock was ticking but, eventually I bought the premises at the rear of Bedfords' original office in Bury that Foffum Developments, the company Sadie and I had set up, had purchased using the money I got from Hamptons! The premises were fine, but we needed a shop window. Following a discussion with Matthew Fullerton, a local commercial agent who had acted for me previously, we secured an attractive small office on the corner of Whiting Street and Langton Place.

When we launched the new business, James and I decided to concentrate on individual, mainly country, properties. With this in mind, we designed the office to present a very comfortable, welcoming environment. We recruited staff who had worked with us previously at Bedfords and subsequently at Hamptons. At my office in Dalham, we employed a secretary/bookkeeper to deal with the administration and accounts. The new business was very well received and, by the summer of 1991, was off to a flying start.

--- ooo ---

To mark the 25th anniversary of the opening of my first office in Swaffham, I was delighted to welcome approximately 150 friends and professional colleagues to a reception at our home, Malting Farm, in Dalham. I was particularly pleased that several members of staff from my very early days in Norfolk managed to attend. Noticing that quite a few partners and agents from other firms were there as well, someone mischievously suggested that, as I was taking a day off, I needed them close at hand – somewhere I could keep my eye on them!

Noel Abel gave a very amusing speech, mixing kind remarks with some embarrassing recollections and the lady who was advertising manager at *Country Life* at the time, Jane Sawyer, presented me with a framed picture in the style of the magazine's renowned *Girls in Pearls* page. For 120 years, this was the place where young ladies announced either that they had found husbands or that they were still looking!

We made good use of the marquee that weekend. The following evening Sadie, who was chairman of Suffolk Ladies' Investment Club that year, held a summer ball and, on the Saturday evening, Michael celebrated his 21st birthday. I clearly remember my reception and Sadie's party going very smoothly, but a small minority of Michael's generation had difficulty in finding pen and paper to confirm whether or not they would attend his party. When the day arrived, we still had no idea if eight or nine of them would turn up. I decided to resolve the problem by making a table plan for all those that had replied, then placing another table in the middle of the dance floor with a large notice that read "For those that did not reply." I received congratulations from quite a few parents afterwards – both of those who had replied and those who hadn't. The culprits were some of the first to reply when it came to other events that year!

--- ooo ---

1991 saw the introduction of *The Property Misdescriptions Act*. It put something of a dampener on the more imaginative descriptions some estate agents occasionally produced. Older readers will remember Roy Brooks' advertisements in *The Sunday Times*. Published in the 1960s, they included such classics as "rundown brothel in Pimlico." This particular piece of legislation was repealed in 2013, to be replaced by *The Consumer Protection Regulations*. It would appear that this new act requires vendors, and more importantly their agents, to disclose virtually any activity in the area that might affect the value of the property. Whether this includes juicy bits of scandal like "Mr A at number 37 visits Mrs B at number 51 every Tuesday afternoon" or not, I have no idea!

Above: "Early learning". George with Paul at prize giving, and

Left: William helping with new board delivery.

Below left: James and I relaunching the business in 1991.

Below right: Michael speaking at Snape on the 10th anniversary of the Aldeburgh office.

RACING, SHOOTING & FISHING.

Top left: Geoffrey Palmer removing a fly from Peter Bucks waders !

Above: "JoJo", one of my dogs that gave me great pleasure.

Left: Sadie and I on a trip to Wales in the 1970s.

Below: The "office" on the Spey.

Right: "Boules" ... lucky to have a share in a horse that won two races.

Below: 1991. The "biggest" ...25 pounder caught on the river Spey

Below right: I enjoyed many trips to Upper Floors on the Tweed at Kelso.

CELEBRATING 25 YEARS – 1991.

Left: Copy of "Bloke with the Pearls" presented by Country Life.

Below: Michael, Sadie, Paul, Me and James relaxing before 150 guests arrived.

Opposite: John Gethin making sure I didn't say anything liable to litigation with fellow agents James Buxton, Jock Lloyd-Jones, Stephen Fletcher and Mark Oliver invited !

Opposite bottom right: Noel Abel with son Tony. Noel was my competitor in 1966, we subsequently became friends. He gave a great speech.

COUNTRY LIFE

SEPTEMBER 6, 1991

MR DAVID BEDFORD
BEDFORD COUNTRY PROPERTY AGENTS

On Friday 6th September 1991, at Malting Farm, David Bedford is holding a celebration of his
25 years in business. Country Life would like to wish him continuing success.

ROLL ON WEDNESDAY...

Like thousands of Country Life readers the first page I turn to when my copy arrives is the Tottering Cartoon.

I sold Annie Tempest the house when she first moved to Norfolk.

Left. Annie and I at an Exhibition of her work which Bedfords were pleased to sponsor.

A surprise present from my sons on my 70th birthday was the framed cartoon, below.

It features "Daffy' and me together with the original board rescued from an outbuilding.

TOTTERING-BY-GENTLY ®

BEDFORD
COUNTRY PROPERTY AGENTS
By appointment
Bury St Edmunds
01284 769999

"...and this is the magnificent triple-aspect open plan kitchen/breakfast room with original Aga..."

Chapter 22

Racing & Rogues

In 1980 – the year before we bought Malting Farm at Dalham – Dalham Hall Estate had sold Dalham Hall Stud, on the edge of Newmarket, to Sheikh Mohammed. The stud's manager had occupied Malting Farm, so it had been excluded from the sale, which is why Sadie and I were able to buy it a year or so later.

While we enjoyed attending the odd Point-to-Point, we weren't all that interested in horse racing but, living just five miles from Newmarket, we attended meetings from time to time and got to know people from the racing world who lived nearby.

I first met John and Lady Carolyn Warren in 1987, when I sold them a small cottage on Fen Ditton Road, Newmarket. Later that year, I attended a sale at Tattersalls one evening, shortly after I sold my business to Hamptons. Cornering me in the bar, Carolyn told me that, now I was a millionaire, I should be buying a horse! Her father was the Seventh Earl of Carnarvon – the Queen's racing manager – and her husband, John, a bloodstock agent. A couple of days later, Carolyn telephoned to say a few friends had bought a horse in the sales and to tell me that, if I was interested in a share, it could be arranged. The members of the syndicate, who included Carolyn and her mother, read like a *Who's Who* of racing. I discussed the idea with Sadie, who thought it would be a good idea – a respite from the pressures of working for Hamptons – so I contacted Carolyn and said we would join.

Over the next year or two, we had many days racing and other trips. The horse, called Boules, was trained by Willie Hastings-Bass, who was later to become Lord Huntingdon. The first race was at Newbury in October 1988 where, together with Carolyn, we enjoyed a wonderful day out. Boules finished second. After the race, we enjoyed tea with Carolyn at her parents' home at Highclere, which is better known these days as Downton Abbey.

A few weeks later, the next trip was to a race at Folkestone where, to everyone's delight, Boules came in first. We were naturally very pleased, but I wondered why Carolyn was so excited. As someone deeply involved in the sport, I assumed she was well-used to horses winning by then. It turned out that only one of her horses had won before, and then only by default. The horse that actually won the race was disqualified on a technicality, so hers had been promoted from second place. Not quite the same!

The following February, our trainer, Willie Hastings-Bass, decided to take Boules and a few other horses from his yard to Cagnes-sur-Mer, in the south of France "to get some sun on their backs." He was well ahead of his time. It was several years later that Arab owners started to transport their horses to Dubai for the winter.

Boules was to participate in a race on the local track, so we spent our three or four days in Cagnes in the company of Carolyn, her parents, Willie's girlfriend and two or three other members of the syndicate. The racing was unusual inasmuch as flat races on the dirt tracks alternated with trotting races, which we had never seen before and have never seen again since! Anticipation was high as the horses lined up at the start, but one horse was particularly tricky and the jockey had great difficulty in getting it into the starting box. I gather from the experts that it should have been disqualified because it obviously unsettled the other horses. Anyway, off they went, and, inevitably, the troublesome horse beat Boules into second place by a nose. It was owned by Sheikh Mohammed.

Racing on the Continent was an eye-opener in as much as the prize money we got when Boules came second in France was considerably more than the combined prize money for the two races we won in England.

Although he had been purchased well by John and had won two races, Boules had still cost us money by the time he was sold. But as it was little more than I would have paid for a gun in a shoot, we had no regrets whatsoever. We had had a most enjoyable time and met some very interesting people.

We were approached on several occasions to join other syndicates, but felt we had been spoilt with our first venture and decided to enjoy racing from a distance in the future.

--- 000 ---

When Lord Carnarvon died in 2001, Carolyn's husband, John, succeeded him as the Queen's racing manager.

I acted for the Warrens in the sale of a couple of houses – the last time being when they left Newmarket to return to Highclere. When Carolyn telephoned to tell me they were leaving, she said that, while a friend had offered to buy the house, they wanted it dealt with at arm's length. Would I act for them? It turned out that the buyer was Michael Stoute, Her Majesty's trainer!

A postscript to this period followed the death of Lord Carnarvon. When he died in 2001, the initial probate valuation for Lake House on Highclere Estate was, I think, carried out by a land agent they had used for many years. A few months later, Carolyn telephoned me to say she wasn't happy with the figure and ask if I would be prepared to help. I said I would, but would need to spend a day or two in the Newbury area to get an idea of prices of comparable properties. She readily agreed, and offered to put my younger son, Michael, and I up while we completed the task. I am pleased to say that we were able to arrive at a figure substantially less than the previous valuation. An important fact had been overlooked. The Seventh Earl of Carnarvon had died at 8pm on 11 September 2001 – the day now known as 9/11. I couldn't imagine that many buyers would have been waving their cheque books at the time, and the valuation office agreed to a substantial reduction in the probate figure. In dying that day, Carolyn's father had been an extremely canny man!

--- ooo ---

Another amusing story involves the Duke and Duchess of Bedford.

As is well known, the family home is the very substantial Woburn Abbey in Bedfordshire but, just down the road from Dalham, they owned a little racing bolt hole – and I do mean little. It was called The Mouse House.

I had met the Duchess briefly when a friend of hers was considering the purchase of a property so, when the time came to sell, she telephoned me and invited me for tea. I went with Diane Tyler, our residential manager. We looked over both the house and the garden, which had wonderful views back towards Dalham. Over tea, we gave the Duchess our thoughts on price and marketing. When she asked us to deal with the sale, the Duke interrupted. "What are we going to tell Bidwells?" he asked. The firm acted as their land agents at Woburn. The Duchess immediately said "No problem! We'll tell them we are using the family firm – Bedfords!"

I duly drafted the sale particulars and sent them to her for approval. The Duchess replied that, while she was very happy with them, she did not approve of the phrase "en suite" that I had included when describing a bathroom. She thought that very middle class. I amended the details to refer to an "adjoining" bathroom instead and have adopted this phrase for country houses ever since.

--- ooo ---

At the other end of the social scale, I am glad to say I was responsible for getting a burglar "put away."

A doctor in West Norfolk asked me to put a substantial country house with several acres on the market. Sometime later, my secretary told me someone wanted to view, but would need to be picked up in Thetford on the Saturday morning. On the drive from Thetford to the property, I asked the prospective buyer where he had come from. He said it was Surrey but that, on that day, he was having his car serviced. I asked where, and he told me at Botwoods in Bury St Edmunds. I knew that, at that time, Botwoods' workshop didn't open on a Saturday, so my suspicions were immediately aroused.

When we arrived at the house, I accompanied him around the property. The owner was away, and there was just an elderly housekeeper in residence. The "buyer" took particular interest in the locks and window latches, explaining to me that he had a lot of valuable paintings and was very security-conscious.

After taking him back to Thetford, I returned to Swaffham, where we were living at the time, and told Sadie all about my day. She said I should contact the police, which I did. I went to the local police station in Swaffham, but no-one there seemed to be very interested. They were in the middle of the investigation on the headless body that had been discovered on Cockley Cley Estate nearby, so I suppose that was understandable. Fortuitously, as I was leaving the station, I bumped into a detective sergeant who I knew as a result of several robberies we had had at the office. He asked what I was doing there, so I told him both about the experience and about the man himself. Following a quick telephone call, it turned out the man was wanted for robbery in the south of England. I told the sergeant he was staying in the Bell Hotel in Thetford overnight. The police arrested him there at about 11 o'clock that evening – ten minutes after the housekeeper at the country house had received a mysterious phone call, presumably from someone checking if the house was occupied. I am pleased to say that the potential burglary was averted. Instead of moving to West Norfolk, the gentleman became Her Majesty's guest for eight years.

--- ooo ---

While on the subject of rogues, there's a story I should tell about one of the loveable kind.

In 1984, I had an interesting thatched farmhouse called Green Farm on the market. Located in Elmswell, the property had attracted a moderate amount of interest when a surveyor – I think he was from London – came to look at it and said he had a client who would like to buy it. It was all very secretive.

It turned out the buyer was the BBC. Green Farm became the headquarters for the crew filming the first series of a programme about a wheeling-dealing trader in antiques called Lovejoy. The house, its grounds, the barn in Preston that we nearly bought before moving to Dalham and other local locations formed the backdrop for the very popular series.

In all, some 71 episodes of Lovejoy were broadcast in six series between 1986 and 1994, but there was a three-year gap between the first and second series. There was a very good reason for this. Based on the success of the first series, which we, like most other people in East Anglia and, indeed, throughout the country, had thoroughly enjoyed, a senior executive of the BBC made an appointment to meet me at Green Farm. To my surprise, he asked me to put a value on the property, which they wanted to put on the market. I had very mixed feelings. The sale would be quite a catch but, on a personal level, I wondered out loud: "Why on earth aren't you having a second series?" He told me that the BBC would have loved to make one at the time, but that the first series had been a joint venture with an Australian company that had failed to produce the money that was due. "There must be a contract you could enforce," I suggested. "Yes, Mr Bedford," he replied. "There was a contract but, unfortunately, the BBC didn't sign it!" The sale of Green Farm was part of the battle the BBC was involved in to get its partners to the negotiating table.

With a slightly heavy heart, I put the property on the market and, eventually, it was sold. It took the BBC three years of legal wrangling before a second series of *Lovejoy* could be made. Unaware of the background, several friends accused me of "killing off" the programme in the meantime!

Chapter 23

Magazines and More

From the early 1980s until Bedfords was sold to Hamptons in 1987, it had produced its own magazine – a fairly modest affair that included a mix of colour and mono pictures. Learning from my time at Hamptons, James and I agreed the new Bedfords should concentrate on quality publications. From 1981, we produced two or three issues of a magazine we called *Country* a year, each with full-colour pages packed with properties, news items and features. Looking through some of the early issues, I remember that, in the summer of 1992, while our business had got off to a flying start in 1991, the first three months of 1992 were some of the worst I had ever experienced. An impending election was unsettling the markets, so very little was coming on to the market.

Despite this, we continued to support various events. The highlight was a gala charity concert held at Tattersalls – a concert by The City of London Sinfonia in aid of The Desert Orchid Farriers Appeal. The capacity audience enjoyed a splendid evening. During the interval, Sadie and I were presented to Her Royal Highness The Princess Royal. Carolyn Warren was her Lady-in-Waiting on that occasion.

--- 000 ---

My elder son, Paul, had been working for Bennetts for seven years by then, selling retirement bungalows. Once Bedfords was established in its new office in Bury St Edmunds, Paul told me he was keen to use the skills had had acquired to exploit what he saw as a growing niche market. As they get older, some people decide they want to move to a bungalow and nothing will persuade them to buy anything else! Paul used the office in Dalham to launch a new firm, Just Bungalows.

Thumbing through the Autumn 1992 issue of *Country*, I was reminded of our sponsorship of Bury St Edmunds' Ladies Hockey Team. Paul had been "walking out" with Kate, the 1st X1 captain, and she telephoned to make an appointment to come to see me in the office. I knew we lived in a changing world, so I wondered if she was coming to ask for permission to marry my son! It turned out that she was wondering whether we would sponsor the hockey team. I told Sadie about the meeting over lunch and she very firmly said "you will sponsor them." She clearly approved of Kate! Whether this clinched matters or not, I'm not sure but, shortly afterwards, Paul and Kate became engaged. They married in 1994.

The 1993 summer edition of *Country* recorded two more important milestones. A gentleman called Henry Pryor had established a club called The London Office to give regional estate agents a greater presence in the capital. By joining, we could promote our clients' properties to a much wider audience. It also gave us an edge when pitching for instructions against national firms like Savills and Knight Frank.

A more important appeal of the arrangement was that Henry Pryor organised a shoot for members. That January, he invited me along. We arrived at a fine country house in Worcestershire and, in the evening, were well fed and watered. The next day, we went shooting.

A guest at the shoot was Suzanne Goldklang, the lady who ran The PR Department, a public relations consultancy based in London. I dined out for some time telling people that I met Suzanne in a ditch! Suzanne did sterling work for several years, securing Bedfords an amazing amount of coverage in the national media.

--- 000 ---

As the Bury office got busier, running it from two premises – Whiting Street for sales and Churchgate Street for administration – was proving an increasing frustration.

I had let Bedfords' original office on the corner of Guildhall Street to an interior decorator. He and his wife were reasonably successful, but he was always inclined to moan about something. He always paid his rent on time, but I sensed that he was struggling. To help both him and me, I suggested that he might like to move up the yard into the offices we had refurbished, which would be at a lower rent. I would release him from his lease on the office I wanted back. The deal was soon agreed.

Bedfords moved back into its original office in February, 1993. We carried out a refurbishment, and it felt like we had never been away. It was good to be back!

My younger son, Michael, had been working with Tony Mullucks who, by then, had re-established himself as a very good agent in Bishop's Stortford. James and I had ideas for expansion, and so it was agreed that Michael would join us in Bury.

The 1994 edition of *Country* contained an article by Thane Prince, *The Daily Telegraph*'s cookery correspondent. Thane was a good friend whom we had known for many years. We got to know her better when she moved from London to Aldeburgh and opened her own cookery school in the town.

Looking through back issues, I am also reminded of opportunities that came to us through Henry Pryor that we mistakenly decided to take a pass on. Among others, there was the chance to sell plots on new a development in Portugal. At "Pinheiros Altos" in the Algarve, plots were on sale at £72,000 at the time. Four bedroom villas with landscaping and pool could be built for around £250,000 – including the plot!

Sadie and I have a week in Algarve most years, which usually includes a ride around some of the developments there. The villas at Pinheiros Altos now sell for between £2 million and £3 million! Twenty years ago, I told those who would listen that £72,000 was a ridiculous price for a plot!

--- ooo ---

Over the six years from 1987 to 1993, there was a sea-change in estate agency.

I had always thought the business quite unsuited to corporate philosophy, but I couldn't afford to walk away from the sort of money Hamptons offered me for my business. As discussed a few chapters ago, banks, building societies and other such institutions had dived headlong into acquiring agents. After leaving Hamptons, I was reported as saying that most of these institutions would withdraw from what, really, had been an "ego trip" – if only because their shareholders would demand it. I thought the 1990s would see the emergence of many more independent firms, and that proved to be the case. The only large corporate chain to survive was Countrywide. "My boy" Harry Hill has retired, and the firm is down to 900 offices from a peak of about 1,100. Firms like William H Brown and Connells have about 300 offices each.

While most of the instructions the new Bedfords received over its first couple of years in business were for properties in West Suffolk, a surprising number came from owners in Mid and North Norfolk. Almost ten years had passed since Bedfords had an office in Norfolk, but the name was clearly still both remembered and respected there.

When James and I looked more closely at where the "over the border" instructions came from, we discovered that the properties concerned were typically just an hour or so from Bury. Importantly, they were about the same distance from Norwich, where many of Norfolk's principal country house agents had their offices. On that basis, we thought more deeply about opening an office to serve the Norfolk market, deciding Burnham Market would be the best location. It took us nearly a year to find premises in the town. Over that time, we could have taken our pick of a dozen premises in King's Lynn, which tells its own story.

The Bower House in Burnham's Market Place had been known for many years as the Fortnum & Mason of North Norfolk. Budge Fitzgerald, the proprietor of the high-class grocery shop, had retired and the premises had been sold, but we managed to secure a lease.

Getting permission to change the use of the premises from a shop to an estate agent's office turned out to be a rather more emotive subject that we had expected. Back then, people saw estate agents as "undesirable" occupants of high streets. These days, they are thought of much more kindly. Today's undesirables are coffee shops, mobile phone, charity and betting shops.

Bearing in mind the "appeal" we thought our arrival would have to the community, we submitted the planning application in the name of our solicitor, but I telephoned one or two councillors to let them know who the user was to be and I was assured of their support. With hindsight, I should have been sceptical. One of those who claimed to be on our side later became a member of a group that national newspapers called the "Turnip Taliban."

When the Council's planning committee met, John Gethin and I sat quietly at the back of the room. When our application came up, the aforesaid member of the "Taliban" presented an excellent case for it to be turned down. Fortunately, Aubrey Haigh, the councillor from King's Lynn, who we had first got to know when Sadie and I performed in *Oklahoma* many years before, explained that we were not just "any old estate agency," but would be offering a quality service. It was a close-run thing, passed just with the chairman's casting vote. Job done, John and I made a deliberately noisy exit. When some of the councillors turned round, they had embarrassed looks on their faces.

We immediately set about refurbishing the premises. The year before, Sadie and I had purchased a holiday home at Burnham Overy Mill, so we were spending quite a bit of time in North Norfolk. The plan was for Michael to run the Burnham office. Thanks to lots of hard work over the first year or two, the new office was a big success. The only problem was that, when the opening day arrived, we hadn't got any staff. In an area that allegedly had high unemployment at the time, recruitment had proved much more challenging than we had expected. To get the show on the road, Michael used his charm to persuade Winkie Mason, a friend from Suffolk, to come and help out for a few weeks.

--- ooo ---

1996 marked the 30th anniversary of the founding of Bedfords in Norfolk.

For the first 16 years, the firm was known as Bedfords – The Estate Agents. After that, it had mostly been known as Bedford Country Property Agents but, over the whole period, the vast majority of friends, clients and colleagues have referred to us simply as Bedfords.

With all three sons now involved in the business, we decided to take the opportunity to update the name to Bedfords.

The year marked a crossroads for Sadie and me as well. They hadn't gone very far, but our boys had all flown the nest. Sadie and I were spending quite a lot of time at our second home in Burnham Market, and the upkeep of our main home, Malting Farm in Dalham, was proving an increasing headache. It had been a wonderful family home, but it sat in seven-and-a-half-acres of grounds, including an acre of formal garden. Several of our friends had sold their houses in the country by then and moved into Bury St Edmunds, and we started to think along the same lines.

At the beginning of the year, I spotted two properties in Angel Lane that, together, would provide an excellent plot on which we could build a new town house. Having embarked on this venture, we put Malting Farm on the market in the summer. It sold fairly quickly. With the new house in Angel Lane only half-built, we put most of our furniture in storage and moved to The Granary at Burnham Overy. Sometimes alone and sometimes with Sadie, I spent two or three nights a week in Bury, enjoying a permanent reservation at an exceptional B&B at 12 Angel Hill. It allowed me to keep in touch with business in Bury and for us to be on the spot to deal with the questions that inevitably arise when a new house is being built.

I have never been too keen on commuting so, in the run-up to Christmas, Sadie and I booked a last-minute trip to Australia. Just after Christmas, we left for six weeks. Optimistically, we hoped that, by the time we got back, the house would almost be ready for occupation.

The development in Angel Lane comprised a main house, which we intended to occupy, and a smaller cottage which, depending on finances, we would either sell or keep and rent out.

We hadn't been back from Australia long when we arranged to meet Joyce Gold, our good friend from Dalham, for a sandwich in The Farmers Club. At the time, she was also looking to move into Bury. She told us she had seen a wonderful property in Garland Street and that she thought we should take a look. Bearing in mind we had two houses under construction in Angel Lane and I had a half-share in four houses that Graham Mothersole and I were refurbishing in Hatter Street, I told Joyce I was what an investor would term "long" on property in Bury and I really didn't want another one. But she was never one to give up. After the sandwich and a couple of drinks, she persuaded Sadie and me to walk round the corner. She put her toe under the gate and lifted it. As the gates swung open, we were confronted by a dreadful 1950s bungalow. Our hearts sank, but then we took in the wonderful third-of-an-acre walled garden in which the property sat. When a doctor had lived next door, it had been his tennis lawn.

I knew immediately that the chance to replace the bungalow with something more appropriate to the location was a once-in-a-lifetime opportunity. Sadie and I had a sleepless night wondering how we could secure the property, which we both wanted. While I was purchasing the site in Angel Lane, Royal Bank of Scotland and I had fallen out over a request for a bridging loan of £60,000 that would have been backed up by property valued in the region of £700,000. In the event, I hadn't needed it – the house in Dalham sold in time – but the disagreement convinced me to switch my account to Lloyds. I made an appointment to see the manager, Roger Tuckett. The property in Garland Street cost £190,000 – it doesn't seem much now, but most of our friends thought we were mad at the time – so, to cover the fees we would have to pay and give us a bit of breathing space, I asked for a loan of £220,000. He said "yes" there and then, and we completed the purchase in early April. Having sold Malting Farm, I was "down" to eight properties – two under construction in Angel Lane, the bungalow in Garland Street, four houses under conversion in Hatter Street and The Granary in Norfolk. Hey ho!

In June, we erected a small marquee in the garden of Garland Lodge so I could celebrate my sixtieth birthday with friends. The 40 who came got the chance to inspect the bungalow in its "before" state and see what we had in mind for the future. Garland Street is part of Bury's central conservation area. Properties nearby were mostly modest, but attractive, Victorian cottages, so it came as a pleasant surprise that the conservation officer was very supportive of our proposals. She even offered to drive a bulldozer to get rid of the "dreadful bungalow."

A friend, Max Millburn, had prepared our plans, but we also have to thank Graham Mothersole for keeping an expert eye on matters of detail as the project progressed.

Simultaneously, we needed to finish off Angel House. Partway through the work there, it would have been virtually impossible to sell. Graham managed to finish the adjoining Stable Cottage off fairly quickly, so Sadie and I moved in there temporarily while Garland Lodge was rebuilt. The plan was to chop the bungalow in half, refurbish the back and build a new Georgian-style wing at the front. Graham drove the project forward and half the property – the back half – was soon ready. It wasn't the finished item, but it did have a sitting room, a kitchen, a bedroom and a bathroom, so we sold Stable Cottage and moved in. Work at Angel House was finished two or three months later. When it sold, we could sleep again at night!

Chapter 24

An Important Handshake

In the summer of 1997, I bumped into Matthew Fullerton, who told me in confidence that clients of his, the Goymer family, owned a substantial block of property in Bury's Hatter Street that they wanted to sell. I can't remember whether there were three or four of them, but the substantial period properties had been converted into about a dozen different apartments, all bar one of which were then empty. I had taken several clients to see the properties, but all had been put off by the amount of work required and, in particular, by the remaining sitting tenant.

A few days later, I met Graham Mothersole in The Farmers Club. He was still working on Garland Lodge at the time. While chatting about property matters, I asked him if he had seen the Hatter Street properties. He had, and thought they could be converted into four good town houses, but was nervous not just about undertaking the project on his own, but about the fact that there was a tenant in residence. I didn't know the lady's name, but it turned out that Graham did. She was a Mrs Hazelton – the mother of a girl called Julia, who I had met through the Young Conservatives in my bachelor days. Julia had married the manager of The Angel Hotel and was then living in Yorkshire.

Mrs Hazelton had run a stationary and bookshop in Abbeygate Street for many years and was the last of three sisters whose maiden name – Groom – was also the name of the shop.

This gave me an idea of how the Hatter Street problem could be solved. Graham thought it would work, so we shook hands on it. If we could buy the properties, we would convert them into four townhouses.

I went back to Matthew Fullerton and agreed a deal under which payment would be staged, but Graham and I would agree to go ahead without planning permission and accept Mrs Hazelton's tenancy. I got Julia's telephone number from a mutual friend and called her in Yorkshire. By then, she had heard that the property had been sold, and was understandably concerned about her mother. Julia was relieved to hear about my involvement and to receive my assurances that we wouldn't be doing what, back then, would have been called a "Rackman." Back in the 1960s, this London landlord became notorious for exploiting his tenants, sometimes forcing them out by taking tiles off their roofs and otherwise rendering properties uninhabitable.

Graham bought a small two-bedroom cottage in Whiting Street and refurbished it. Julia was delighted and moved her mother there, where she remained for several years.

We obtained planning permission and progressively developed the site into four fine townhouses, which had gardens and parking areas approached from Churchgate Street.

--- ooo ---

To facilitate the Hatter Street development, Graham and I formed a company called Madebid. The directors were Graham and Linda Mothersole, Sadie and I, but we never felt it necessary to have a formal partnership agreement. A handshake in the Farmers Club in Bury St Edmunds was good enough for us!

When we identified a project, each of us would put, say, £100,000 into the company to cover the costs, with a facility being arranged with the bank to cover the balance. Graham's company would build the properties and Bedfords would sell them. Depending on the scale of the project and the time scale, we would each put in an equal additional amount if further capital was required. This arrangement with Graham and I worked extremely well.

Some of Madebid's most successful developments were those it completed within Bury St Edmunds' historic centre. They included a fine new Georgian-style house adjoining St Marys Church in Honey Hill. Madebid also built four new houses and converted a property in Church Row – a project that involved buying parts of the site from three different owners. Apart from being financially rewarding, I would like to think the developments provided attractive additions to the town.

--- ooo ---

While on the subject of the Goymers – the family who owned the properties in Hatter Street – I remember having met Martin Goymer's father in my days at Rutters. It was in the 1950s, when I used to open the firm's Mildenhall office on Tuesdays and Fridays.

There was a large US air-force base nearby at the time. Most of the personnel there was American and, while refrigerators were a very expensive luxury in Britain back then, no self-respecting American family could exist without one.

As I was sitting in the office in Mildenhall one afternoon, a green van drew up. It had "Rent-A-Fridge" painted on the side. Martin's father – I think he was called Harold – came in, introduced himself and explained that he rented fridges, mainly to Americans, for what I think was two shillings (10p) a week. This might not sound very much, but it turned out that he had an awful lot of fridges out on rent. With there being 52 weeks in every year, this clever enterprise earned enough to allow him to buy properties in the area, which he also rented out to Americans. At one stage, I think his empire owned several hundred properties in Beck Row, Lakenheath and Weeting.

The Goymers still own an extensive portfolio of properties, but Martin decided to "diversify." Many years ago, he decided to develop the family fruit farm at Banham into a zoo. It became a hugely successful tourist attraction. From acorns, mighty oak trees grow!

--- ooo ---

The work on the houses in Hatter Street continued into 1998.

That September, Graham completed the work on Garland Lodge, and Sadie and I moved in.

With the completion and sale of the Hatter Street properties, Sadie and I now had a much more manageable portfolio of just two houses – Garland Lodge and The Granary at Burnham Overy Staithe.

We were still spending a fair amount of time in Norfolk, where Michael, who had joined the partnership in 1997, was increasingly taking full responsibility for the Burnham Market office.

Bedfords had opened a Just Bungalows branch in my original office at 95 Market Place in Swaffham by then. Given the hundreds of bungalows I had sold in Swaffham and the surrounding villages, it was a natural extension of the Bury St Edmunds office. Paul had identified an ideal man to manage the office in Swaffham – a chap called Brian Lofthouse, who had spent many years with Charles Hawkins & Sons, lived locally and was keen to join us. A very active, personable, middle-aged man, he was ideal for the retired bungalow market. There was a touch of nostalgia about the official opening, which was performed by John Alan, the managing director of Anglia Newspapers. When I had first opened an office there, he had been the young advertising executive for *The Lynn News* who took the order for my first advertisement. John gave me a framed copy at the opening.

For the first few months, the new venture really took off, but tragedy struck early in the summer when Brian suffered a heart attack and died. The respect people in the profession had for him was obvious from the very large congregation at his funeral. Held in Fincham Church, it was attended by many former colleagues from Hawkins, local solicitors and others connected with the business.

We never found a way to replace Brian at the Swaffham office, which left Paul under a great deal of pressure. Towards the end of 1999, we bowed to the inevitable and closed the office down. We thought the offices in Bury and Burnham Market would adequately be able to cater for country properties in Mid Norfolk, and we were right. It continues to be the case.

Above: One of my favourite ads ...this century!

Chapter 25

The New Millennium

Come New Year's Eve at the end of 1999, Sadie and I, together with many of our friends, were guests at Croxton Park, the home of John and Melinda Raker. The wonderful party culminated in a firework display over the beautiful grounds.

Business in North Norfolk had been growing rapidly, and we had recruited Andrew Pointon – the cousin of Chris Pointon, my former partner at Swaffham. Chris had bravely been fighting cancer for some time by then, and finally succumbed to the dreadful illness in 2001.

Thinking that Michael might move back to Suffolk over the next year or two, we also decided to look for an experienced potential partner to manage Burnham. Andrew was understandably disappointed, but we parted on amicable terms. After working for a couple of agents in Holt, he established his own successful business.

We interviewed several applicants for the post in Burnham, one of whom was a very confident judge's son who ended up interviewing us! Subsequent events proved us right in declining his offer to run our business! After much debate, we finally settled on Andrew Wagstaff, a chartered surveyor in his mid-fifties who had many years' experience with Hanbury Williams in Norwich and, more recently, at an office in Holt.

We hadn't planned to move Michael back to Bury immediately, but the decision was made for us. Having been given 12 points following various offences, my son lost his driving licence. It's hard for an agent to sell houses in a rural area if he can't drive!

The partners decided to give Michael the sabbatical he wanted to travel to Australia via India. In the early hours of 11 September 2001, a car turned up to take him to the airport. As he left, I told him to "make sure you ring mother when you get there."

Michael's Volkswagen Golf had done a high mileage, and I had offered to take it to the local dealership in Bury St Edmunds to get a price for it. We would sort another car out for him when he got his driving licence back. On the way to the garage, I heard about a plane crash on the car radio. Naturally, my heart missed a beat! I returned home just in time to see a second plane crashing into the Twin Towers in New York. None of us will forget that fateful day!

The drama was being played out over the skies of America, but we inevitably wondered if it was a worldwide terrorist operation. When Michael finally rang at midnight, we were much relieved! There hadn't been any announcements about the attacks on Michael's British Airways flight – they probably didn't want to upset the passengers – so he learnt the news from a taxi driver taking him to his hotel in Delhi. The repercussions of 9/11 and the turmoil in the Middle East that followed are still with us.

--- ooo ---

By the time Michael got back from his trip, Andrew was well established running the core country-property practice in Norfolk, so Michael was able to return to Bury St Edmunds.

Burnham Market had been a great success for Bedfords, and I felt there was a similar opportunity for the business in East Suffolk – particularly in the sought-after area including Southwold, Aldeburgh and Woodbridge.

While Sadie and I were spending a very pleasant weekend with Michael and Hilary Haydon at their home in Thorpeness, we drove into Aldeburgh on the Saturday evening. There, I noticed an office occupied by an old, established firm called Tughy. Mike told me Mr Tughy wasn't enjoying the best of health and was thinking of retiring. I made an appointment to see him a week later. He told me that, yes, he was considering retirement but, despite several useful meetings with him, he decided to carry on for the time being. He sold very few properties – his main business was letting and holiday cottages – so we told him we would probably pursue opening an office in Aldeburgh independently. He fully understood.

Paul, James, Michael and I spent half a day in Aldeburgh a few weeks later and, clearly, our presence was noted. Soon afterwards, I received a letter from a partner at a local agent, explaining that there was very little business in Aldeburgh and that several other firms that had looked into the opportunity had decided in the end not to open there. We saw this as confirmation that there definitely was an opportunity in the town!

As a courtesy, I telephoned the chap who had sent me the letter. He proceeded to pour more cold water on our proposed opening. I had discovered that he spent most of his time at Aldeburgh Golf Club, where I expect he did quite a bit of business so, having listened to his tale of woe, I asked "Well, would you like to sell your Aldeburgh office?" He quickly ended the call!

Far from put off, we rented a temporary office in Aldeburgh. Early in 2003, Michael moved to East Suffolk to take charge and manage the launch. It was a new area for us, so business took longer to build up than it had done in Burnham Market, where the reputation my original firm had built up gave us a flying start.

--- 000 ---

Andrew Wagstaff had accepted the invitation to join the partnership at Burnham Market, but the office there became even busier, so he recruited a manager, Ben Marchbank, to help.

The year finished with a flourish. The feel-good factor that followed Johnny Wilkinson's dropped goal and the winning of the Rugby World Cup in November helped but, given the team's performance since, that now seems an awfully long time ago!

Towards the end of the 1990s, Bedfords joined Mayfair Office, an organisation that Nick Churton had set up to give regional estate agents a presence in the capital.

While we had enjoyed being with The London Office, Henry Pryor was spending an increasing amount of his time working with the media on property matters. The final straw came when he told us the subscription was going up and, at the same time, he would be closing the office in Berkeley Square. He couldn't tell us where the new premises would be!

Nick proved to be very pro-active. Mayfair Office has excellent contacts with the national media, so Bedfords punches above its weight when it comes to getting coverage for the properties on its books. The only downside is that, unlike Henry, he doesn't arrange a shoot. The annual dinner is very convivial, though. Held in The RAF Club in London, it's where Bedfords and other like-minded members get to meet.

Chapter 26

Always a Tractor Boy

Even while we were living in Norfolk in the late 1970s, I would go to Portman Road several times a season to see matches. Friends who had season tickets or, in one case, a box were generous with invitations to see Ipswich Town in action. The highlight came when I got the chance to see Ipswich beat Arsenal 1-0 in the FA Cup Final at Wembley in 1978. But it wasn't until about the time we moved to Dalham that I became a regular supporter. It all started when Paul Rackham loaned me his two season tickets, which were for seats in a prime position in Block D – on the halfway line, halfway up the stand. He told me I could hold onto the tickets provided he could have them back when he needed them. For a season or two, I bought him a nice case of wine at Christmas by way of a thank-you but, in the end, I told him "You really must let me pay for these tickets." Eventually, he agreed on condition that, if he ever wanted them back, I would release them. Paul always wanted to keep his options open! Some 25 years later, after he had sold his waste business for £400 million and he and his family had a box of their own at Portman Road, I asked "Do you really want the tickets back?" With a wry smile, he answered "No. I think you can keep them!"

And so it was that I was lucky enough to enjoy the final seasons of the Bobby Robson era from an excellent vantage point at Portman Road. After he left to manage to England, Ipswich

Town had three full-time managers before, under George Burley, they made it into the Premiership in 2000. The 4-2 win over Barnsley made another trip to Wembley one I will never forget.

Town's first season in the Premiership was a memorable one. Although I'm not a betting man, I was fired with enough enthusiasm and hope at the beginning of the season to visit Corals' betting shop in Abbeygate Street, Bury St Edmunds. Apart from me, the only people in the shop were the two assistants behind the counter. I asked what odds Corals were offering on Ipswich winning the Premiership. The assistants looked at me in astonishment. After a telephone call to head office, they confirmed the odds at the time were 2500 to 1. I calmly peeled off five £20 notes and placed them on the counter, which prompted another call to head office. Eventually, whoever was at the other end of the line agreed to the bet. I was convinced I'd be walking out in May of the following year with a cheque for £250,000.

By Christmas, Ipswich were third in the league and those of my friends who know much more about betting than I were telling me I could sell the ticket back to Corals for a profit. Unfortunately, I decided to hold onto it. Come the end of the season, it still looked like Town could finish third. Martin Lightfoot, who eagerly shared the tickets with me, agreed we should go to the last game against Derby – an away match. Unfortunately, we lost and finished fifth. I didn't make my £250,000, but it was still an amazing result. The following year, Town would be playing in the UEFA Cup!

The first leg of the opening match against Inter Milan was played at Portman Road. Ipswich won 1-0, so Graham Mothersole, who occasionally accompanied me to matches, and I decided to take a trip to Italy for the second leg a couple of weeks later. Ipswich's allocation of seats and other packages had all been sold but the son of a great friend of ours, Jack Gold, was – and indeed still is – a senior executive with Nike, so I telephoned him to ask if he could get us any tickets. As Nike sponsored Inter Milan, he said this wouldn't be a problem. The tickets would be some of the best seats in the ground. All I had to do was collect them from a young lady called Yumi.

The package flights were all sold, so – reluctantly! – we decided to fly business class to Milan with Alitalia. To complete our travel arrangements, Jack arranged for us to stay in the same hotel as Ipswich Town's squad and officials.

Arriving at the ground, we met Yumi, who handed us the tickets and passes we needed. Upon entry into what was clearly the executive lounge, Graham and I felt a bit under-dressed compared to the crowd of extremely wealthy and immaculately dressed Italians, but we enjoyed the amazing hospitality nonetheless. Having spotted us in the room, John Kerr, one of the Ipswich Town directors I knew well, came over and asked "What are you two buggers doing here?" Aside from the directors of the two teams, I suspect many of those present were Mafiosi with whom Inter Milan were reputed to be connected at the time.

When the time came for the match to start, we were handed programmes and escorted to our seats by a liveried official who, just before our bums hit our seats, placed cushions under us. Unfortunately, Ipswich lost 4-1 – 4-2 on aggregate – but we enjoyed the trip enormously. Before catching the plane home the next day, Graham suggested we buy our wives presents. Looking around, we lighted on a very expensive handbag shop. Looking at one, Graham asked the assistant how much it cost. Thinking the price he was given was in pounds rather than in Lira, he looked as though he might have a heart attack. "Christ!" he spluttered, "I could buy a building plot for that!" The assistant quickly converted the price from Lira into Sterling but, even so, the bag was still quite expensive.

--- ooo ---

Over the years, I have been asked to help several Ipswich Town managers to find houses in Suffolk. I remember in particular John Lyle, who was charming, and Roy Keane, who, while not quite charming, was very interesting and agreeable – nothing like his public persona. I showed Keane and his wife several properties and was impressed by how down-to-earth they both were. It turned out he has an amazing memory. I met him in Aldeburgh to show him over a property the day after a pre-season match Town played against a Spanish side. While we were looking around, he asked if I had been to the match. "Yes," I said, "with my grandson, who's a Norwich fan, and an exchange student who is Spanish!" Some months later, I was invited to a season ticket-holders' event. When Keane came into the room, he came straight up to me with a very large smile on his face and asked if my grandson was still supporting Norwich. Bearing in mind how well Norwich were doing compared to Ipswich, I replied "What do you think!"

Unfortunately, Keane never succeeded in turning Ipswich Town's fortunes around and neither did his successor.

Mick McCarthy has done a good job in rescuing us from potential relegation and taking us to the playoffs in May 2015. The current season started well but has run out of steam with many supporters dismayed at the "Sunday morning park" long ball style of play. As I write this I am not sure if I or indeed Mick McCarthy will be at Portman Road next season!

May 2nd 2016

Tomorrow is the final deadline for my book, but all football fans will remember it as the day they woke up to learn history was made by Leicester City winning the Premier League. A team who also play in Blue came tantalisingly close in 2001... Well done Leicester.

Chapter 27

Bury St Edmunds'
Best-Kept Secret

Bury St Edmunds has always been regarded as a very pleasant market town. Well situated in the middle of East Anglia – within easy reach of Cambridge, Ipswich and Norwich – it isn't quite accessible enough to have become a base for people who want to commute every day to London.

Surprisingly, it wasn't until it launched a Millennium Appeal for funds to complete its tower that many outside East Anglia realised the town had a cathedral. Prince Charles became the Patron for the appeal, which ensured it got a lot of publicity. Thanks to a legacy from the architect, Stephen Dykes Bower, various grants and more than £3 million raised locally, the £10 million needed was eventually raised and work started.

In 2004, several invited guests and I got the chance to see the work in progress. Organised by Graham Mothersole, the "hard hat" tour took us up the tower in the contractor's lift to get a close-up view of the amazing work the craftsmen had done.

It wouldn't be until 2010 that the fan-vaulted ceiling under the roof of the new tower would be completed but an interesting by-product of the project was that, in the early years of the new millennium, more and more of those coming to Bedfords' office were clearly looking not just for properties in the town, but for a property anywhere that had a cathedral. "We have been to York," they would tell us. "Next week, we're going to Salisbury." As those who bought on this basis will know by now, Bury has much more to offer!

--- ooo ---

As a family, we were horrified when we heard the dreadful news of the tsunami on Boxing Day, 2004.

When we lived in Swaffham, we saw a lot of Mike and Jane Cornwall. Their three daughters were similar in age to our three boys, and we had many happy times there together. I remember in particular summer days we spent around our swimming pool at Holmwood.

By 2004, the Cornwall's elder daughter, Louise, had married. That Christmas, she, her husband Nigel and four children had gone on holiday to Thailand. On the way to the beach on 31 December, Louise had called in at a small supermarket to get some sun cream. It was then that the tsunami hit, sweeping the building away in its path.

Her husband and children survived, but Louise's death had a huge effect on the younger generation in Norfolk – much as the DC10 crash had done in the case of our generation some 30 years earlier.

--- ooo ---

Bedfords continued to flourish.

In 2005, the Bury St Edmunds office was extended and refurbished and staff including Emmerson Dutton and Rosanna Percival were recruited.

In 2006, we celebrated the 40th anniversary of the founding of the firm with parties at The Athenaeum in Bury St Edmunds and in the firm's office in Burnham Market. At both events, Penny Churchill, the property correspondent for *Country Life*, said a few words – some embarrassing and some complimentary!

I was very pleased that, despite his advancing years, Peter Hart managed to get along to one of the events. He spent quite a long part of the evening in deep conversation with Harry Hill. I'm not sure what they talked about, but Harry told me afterwards that he'd learnt a lot!

I would have liked Brian Cross to have been at the party in Burnham Market but, as I mentioned in chapter 15, he died a few days earlier. I was very conscious of his absence.

In 2007, Bedfords launched a new-style property magazine. The editorial in the first issue included a reference to another tsunami – the one we thought would hit the market the following year. "Whilst there may be an increase in repossessions," it said, "we foresee no likelihood of a crash similar to the late 1980s." How wrong we were!

A reference was made to a government enquiry to be launched into the property market, on which I commented "On the few occasions when prices have come down, it's been due to events well outside the influence of any government!"

The events of 2008 are still remembered by most in the property business. That spring, Sadie and I heard from Harry Hill's wife Mandy, who was arranging a surprise 60th birthday party in Portugal. It was attended everyone from the corporate agency world, including movers and shakers from John D. Wood, Connells, Rightmove and Countrywide. The unanimous opinion was that, business-wise, the year would be a write-off, but we all had a splendid weekend. In the speech I made, I outlined Harry's desire to build a chain and my wish to develop a small, personal business. Countrywide had 1,100 offices at the time, compared to Bedfords' three, so I guess we both got what we wanted. We were certainly both happy with the decisions we had made, but several of those present confided in me after the speech that they thought I was on the right track!

--- ooo ---

Over my years in the property business, I had experienced several recessions. Then, the market had slowly dimmed – a bit like someone turning down the lights. 2008 was very different. The lights literally went out overnight!

Bedfords' business halved, leaving the partners in a very difficult position. To keep the business afloat, they not only had to make cuts to the amounts they drew from the business – some had to remortgage their homes to give the firm sufficient capital to operate. I was no longer a partner by then, but I was happy to help out.

In my time in the business, we had never had to make anybody redundant or give anyone the sack. More by luck than by judgment, we didn't have to this time either. While emergency meetings were going on, our two chief negotiators, Rosanna Percival and Paula Reynolds, simultaneously decided they wanted to work in London to gain more experience – I'm not quite sure of what! The partners shed crocodile tears when they left, but they weren't replaced. We were also helped by Di Tyler, our residential manager, who was approaching retirement. She happily agreed to a redundancy package with a nod and a wink that we would re-employ her part-time when conditions improved. We did, and she is still with us.

Combined with ruthless cuts in overheads – did we really need those water coolers? – the firm's cost base was cut enough to ensure its survival, but 2008 was the worst year it had ever endured. Bedfords was lucky, though. With the number of property transactions across Britain down 35 percent, estate agencies were closing offices all around us. Despite its promise, the Government's plan to require sellers to produce Home Information Packs (HIPs) did nothing to help. There were real problems, of course, but, with the media constantly feeding the population bad news, the recession soon became a self-fulfilling prophecy.

It was during this period that anonymous letters started to arrive again, relishing the possibility that the firm and I, in particular, might be facing ruin. We were delighted to disappoint them! The firm survived what turned out to be a relatively short difficult period, the following year producing an all-time record profit.

--- 000 ---

For several years, The Bank of England held regional meetings to gather information on the economy.

Twice a year, I was invited to the Bank in London to give "grass roots" information on the property market. At one of the *BBC Question Time*-style events, the Bank's property "expert" trotted out figures produced by the Halifax and the Nationwide Building Societies. For reasons I have explained previously, I think figures like those are pretty meaningless in the context of the overall market. When the microphone was handed to me, I asked the expert if she knew what percentage of property transactions involved no mortgage at all. She couldn't give me an answer so I told her that, nationwide, it was 35 percent. I can still remember the expression on her face! She clearly had no idea so much of the market was below the lenders' radar. In recent years, the figure has increased, making lenders' statistics even less relevant. At Bedfords, it is now somewhere in the region of 65 percent.

--- 000 ---

Early in 2009, the market suddenly woke up. Over the spring and early summer of that year, sales through Bedfords' offices doubled compared with 2008, but the media was still talking about the market "spiralling downwards." In the editorial of our

2009 magazine, my son, Paul, referred to "a warmer breeze blowing through the market compared with some areas" but, in reality, our experience was being echoed by many regional agents. We were particularly lucky to receive some very good instructions and, amazingly, 2009 turned out to be the most profitable year the firm had ever enjoyed. The partners and their families were able to sleep again at night and my loan was repaid. Rosanna decided to return to Suffolk and Bedfords was delighted to welcome her back to what, by then, was once again a very busy office.

The only disappointment was that, early that December, Emmerson Dutton came to see me at home on a Sunday evening to say that he had decided to set up an office on his own. I thought he had a future with the firm at the highest level, so I told him I was very disappointed to hear about his plans. It turned out that he had a financial backer, so there was little point in trying to dissuade him, but I warned him that arrangements like that very rarely worked out. We shook hands and I wished him well, telling him he knew where I was if he ever wanted to have a chat in the future.

--- ooo ---

The turn-around in the market in 2009 defied the underlying economic situation and wasn't predicted by even the most eminent of commentators. In East Anglia, it was as if the credit crunch and the demise of the global financial markets had never happened.

Those who needed either just a relatively small mortgage requirement or none at all returned to the market in sufficient numbers to outstrip the supply of suitable properties. This left many buyers surprised by the return of competitive bidding and exasperated by the lack of stock meeting their criteria.

We will all remember 2010 for different reasons. Among the noteworthy events that year were the launch of the iPad, the engagement of Prince William and the creation of the first coalition government in almost 70 years.

The early part of the year had been dominated by the harshest winter in over 30 years. Taken together with the announcement of a General Election, this reduced the activity in the property market for a while but confidence returned, after the Election, albeit at a more modest pace.

Over the years since I retired, Bedfords has gone from strength to strength. The recipe I established of concentrating on traditional strengths and both employing and retaining quality staff has continued to work well.

Anonymous "fan mail", 2008.

Chickens are coming home to roost Bedford. Look forward to reading about another Estate Agent closing. If anyone deserves to suffer its you.

Chapter 28

Sixty Years

I freely admit that, these days, I've become a fully paid-up grumpy old man.

In the spring of 1987, when I bought a new BMW 7 series from him, my pal Peter Buck told me that the latest "must have" item was a car phone. My recollection is that the car cost about £25,000, to which the phone added another £1,800! The handset was fitted between the front seats, but another substantial box of tricks was fitted in the boot. I transferred it into a couple of subsequent cars, after which my son, Paul, had it installed in his Golf for several years. From the point of view of the reliability and reception, it was excellent, but technology has moved on, of course. These days, almost everyone has a mobile phone or tablet, preferably the latest model.

For something like 25 years, I had a succession of very basic Nokia phones that, even though they couldn't get me to the moon and back, were excellent for sending and receiving a text and telephone calls.

Some years ago at a wedding, I found myself sitting next to Charles Dunston, the founder of Carphone Warehouse. I had met him many years previously when he bought a house in Burnham Market and, inevitably, we got chatting about our respective businesses. I produced my Nokia phone and asked him if there was any good reason why I should change it. I wondered if anything was likely to go wrong with it. After a furtive glance around the table, he whispered that nothing would!

The number of families these days who sit silently in restaurants, playing with their electronic devices, never ceases to amaze me. Mum, dad and two or three kids – they are all at it. No wonder the art of conversation is in danger of extinction!

Recently, Sadie and I spent four nights in Vienna with another couple. After visiting a restaurant, we decided to walk the half-mile back to the hotel through the main pedestrianised street. It was a Friday night, so it was very busy. There must have been several thousand people walking in the opposite direction, and it suddenly struck me that nobody was on a phone. They were all engaging in happy conversation. I alerted my friend Richard, and we carefully scanned everyone we passed. Just before we reached the hotel, we saw one – yes, just one – young girl on her phone. In Bury St Edmunds, Norwich, London or wherever, the situation would quite probably be the reverse, with only one person not on a phone.

It's because of this that, while driving down Abbeygate Street in Bury St Edmunds one day, I nearly came a cropper. The street is pedestrianised until 4pm, but this was at about 4.30pm. Some 30 to 40 yards (27 to 37m) ahead, I spotted a guy walking towards me in the middle of the road, intently studying his phone. I slowed down and waited until he was about four feet from my bonnet, then gave him a blast on my horn. Much to the amusement of pedestrians who thought he was about to walk into my car, he jumped about two feet in the air. Needless to say, he went berserk, but I had taken the precaution of locking the doors.

--- ooo ---

Paul has been successful not only in developing the new homes business, but also taking over from me as managing partner of a very large business covering Suffolk and most of Norfolk.

Over the years, he and his wife, Kate, have been very involved with Bury St Edmunds Hockey Club. Kate represented England Masters on a tour of Australia and their children, Oscar, Molly and George, have all followed in their parents' and grandfathers' footsteps, playing hockey at various levels. As I write this, Oscar is enjoying his second year at Manchester Metropolitan University studying Business Management, Molly is about to take her A Levels and George, still only 13, has become a keen sportsman. In a recent game of golf, his grandad came a poor second!

Over the 2015/16 New Year, Paul and his family took the opportunity to visit the memorial to my father at Casino while staying in Rome. My grandson, Oscar, who was 19 at the time, was upset to see how many of his age had died there, including several who shared his birthday. When he got back, it was my turn to get emotional. At 34 – nearly twice the age of most of his mates – my Dad need never have gone to war. It upset Mother so much.

James was with me at the birth of the current business in 1991 and has been very successful in growing the country property business in Suffolk. He has a long-term partner of 20 years, Rebecca. Her children – Tom, Frankie and Henry – are now grown-up. Although James and Rebecca aren't married, it is very comforting to see what a happy family unit they are.

Credit for the setting up of the branch offices must go to Michael. More than 20 years have passed since he was first sent to Burnham Market – the "colonies" as we put it. Since then, he has moved to East Suffolk to open the offices in Aldeburgh and, more recently, in Woodbridge. Michael lives in Thorpeness with his two lovely children William and Bella.

I have often been asked how the family survived with both me and all three sons working in the same business. Earlier, I described how my "empire" days came to an end. I am told the boys found me a difficult act to follow, but they do it extremely well. Sadie also helped a great deal, insisting that business and family life were kept separate. With advancing years, I hope I have learnt not to interfere – well, not too much, anyway!

--- ooo ---

Many of those I've worked with have felt like "family" as well.

Before closing, I would also like to give updates about a few of those mentioned in this book.

In addition to his excellent work ethic, I have been very grateful for Andrew Wagstaff's help and support, particularly in "father vs. sons" debates. He was the first non-family partner at Bedfords.

Ben Marchbank became a partner in 2012. He has had a very successful career with us and is recognised as one of North Norfolk's most experienced and well-respected agents.

After a chance meeting with Paul in the summer of 2014, Emmerson Dutton returned to Bedfords, accepting an invitation to join the partnership, merging his business with ours.

In Bury St Edmunds, Diane Tyler still plays a pivotal role as a part-time progressor of sales that lie in the hands of solicitors. With her knowledge and experience, solicitors are always ready to take a call from Diane, as they know it will be a relevant question to be dealt with.

Although officially retired from the partnership since 2003, I have been very happy to be involved in strategic decisions since then and also, from time to time, in advising long-standing clients and friends.

Andrew has recently dropped down to part-time, but Ben Marchbank has successfully stepped up and the Burnham Market office continues to thrive with a new team. With Emmerson Dutton having joined the partnership at its Bury office and Paul acting as managing partner, the firm's future is in good hands as it approaches its 50th birthday.

The "second half" that started in 1991 certainly hasn't been a disappointment. All three of my sons eventually joined the firm, and I am immensely proud of how it has developed under their stewardship.

With the further partners who have joined the firm in recent years, it still retains the values of a family firm. A new office has recently been opened in Woodbridge, which works closely with the Aldeburgh office, strengthening Bedfords' position in East Suffolk.

--- ooo ---

Writing this in the summer of 2015 – 60 years after I got my first job – provided me with an opportunity to reflect on how Britain has changed over that time, and how the property business has changed with it.

From Harold Wilson to David Cameron, prime ministers have come and gone. The socialists didn't get everything wrong and the conservatives didn't get everything right, and it didn't have much of an impact on the property market either way. There is really only one thing that has mattered – supply and demand. Governments have tinkered and tried to influence the market, but the things that have most influenced the numbers and prices of houses being built and sold have been the economy and events – national and international.

The biggest problem – one that has been around for many years and only seems to get worse – is the question of supply. We are, I'm afraid, a nation of "nimbies." It saddens me to see generations that have enjoyed full employment and the growth in property values and indirectly, in their pensions form protest groups to oppose virtually every planning application for new housing. In recent months, for example, photographs in local newspapers have shown about 40 or 50 middle-aged residents celebrating a council's refusal of plans for new houses that its planning department had recommended for approval. In the vast majority of cases, local authorities incur big fees fighting appeals, which they almost inevitably lose.

A recent article in *The Sunday Times* by Luke Johnson provided an excellent definition of the nimby disciples:

> *"Facilitators of decay in our surroundings, this volunteer breed are mainly engaged in preserving the past, stopping property development at all cost. They hunger to have Britain frozen as a twee period piece – damn the prospects for the young, job creation and industry. They are small minded, selfish and hypocritical, spending their lives objecting to anything to do with change."*

Hysterical campaigns mounted by prominent individuals and organisations like The National Trust have suggested that the whole of England's green and pleasant land will be built upon if planners get their way.

The problem is that local councillors – most of whom do a good job – come under enormous pressure when it comes to planning decisions. It seems to me as though the situation would be much improved if the government transferred the responsibility for the work to county councils that could act more strategically. Thirty-year-olds would then be less likely to see their dreams of home ownership torpedoed by their parents, grandparents and neighbours.

Postscript

Over the past 60 years, the estate agency business has seen dramatic changes, particularly as a result of technologies introduced over the last ten to 15 years.

As well as enjoying the good times, the firm I founded has weathered various storms. I was particularly pleased when an article in *The Daily Telegraph*'s property supplement named Bedfords "one of the top 20 independent estate agents in Britain." The firm might only just be marking its 50th birthday, but there seems little reason why it shouldn't be celebrating its centenary in 2066.

From time to time, I wonder what I would have done if I had not accepted the job the Youth Employment Office in King's Lynn offered me all those years ago. I put the success I have achieved down to the fact that I have really enjoyed working in the business. Some might say I've been lucky – and I have – but I recently came across a quotation attributed to Seneca, the Roman philosopher who was tutor and then advisor to the emperor, Nero, that seems to sum it up:

"Luck is what happens when preparation meets opportunity."

ABSENT FRIENDS

The seat at the bottom of our beautiful garden is where I sometimes sit and reflect on my three score years and ten, plus a few more.

I think of those that are no longer with us including family, staff and many dear friends. Some I have mentioned in this book - "property remains but none of us are immortal."

Sadie and I at Home April 2016.

Granny's
Boasting Book

FAMILY – EASTER 2016
Above: Oscar, Katie, James, Rebecca, Molly, Sadie, Paul, Me and George.
Below: William, Bella and Michael.

David Bedford

"...ONE OF THE TOP 20 INDEPENDENT ESTATE AGENTS IN BRITAIN"

The Daily Telegraph

Left: The first fifty years.
Below: ...Leading the firm forward!

Paul Bedford

Michael Bedford

James Bedford

Ben Marchbank

Andrew Wagstaff

Emmerson Dutton